ANCIENT
SPIRIT WISDOM

ANCIENT
SPIRIT WISDOM

AN ELDER'S GUIDEBOOK TO NATIVE
SPIRITUALITY AND BEYOND

IlgaAnn "Spider Spirit Woman" Bunjer, MSW

BALBOA.
PRESS
A DIVISION OF HAY HOUSE

Balboa Press books may be ordered through booksellers or by contacting:

Balboa Press
A Division of Hay House
1663 Liberty Drive
Bloomington, IN 47403
www.balboapress.com
1-(877) 407-4847

Because of the dynamic nature of the Internet, any web addresses or links contained in this book may have changed since publication and may no longer be valid. The views expressed in this work are solely those of the author and do not necessarily reflect the views of the publisher, and the publisher hereby disclaims any responsibility for them.

The author of this book does not dispense medical advice or prescribe the use of any technique as a form of treatment for physical, emotional, or medical problems without the advice of a physician, either directly or indirectly. The intent of the author is only to offer information of a general nature to help you in your quest for emotional and spiritual well-being. In the event you use any of the information in this book for yourself, which is your constitutional right, the author and the publisher assume no responsibility for your actions.

Any people depicted in stock imagery provided by Thinkstock are models, and such images are being used for illustrative purposes only.
Certain stock imagery © Thinkstock.

ISBN: 978-1-4525-3341-4 (sc)
ISBN: 978-1-4525-3343-8 (hc)
ISBN: 978-1-4525-3342-1 (e)

Library of Congress Control Number: 2011904373

Printed in the United States of America

Balboa Press rev. date: 4/21/2011

Ann's book, Ancient Spirit Wisdom: An Elder's Guidebook to Native Spirituality and Beyond, is a wonderful synthesis of how to connect to what has heart and meaning in life. She honors the wisdom of the ancestors, yet teaches now to live fully in the present. She teaches the old sacred methods of personal and communal ritual in a way that is simple, direct and accessible to all. There is something for everyone who is wanting to bring their life into balance with the universe and spirit. While she teaches the specific meaning of various ceremonies she is also gently giving a world view that can help integrate a person into the divine whole.

Ann's personal journey growing up in Europe during World War 2 has given her strength and personal integrity that is obvious to those who know her. That harsh beginning allows her to see the true value of living in balance with the earth, humans and all creatures of nature. This is a great beginning book for those starting their metaphysical journey and a good refresher course for those on their way.

Shanti Toll
Owner/Director, Clebration Productions Fair

"Ancient Spirit Wisdom prepares each of us as we approach the Mayan predicted Shift in 2012. This book has a beautiful way of combining spiritual ritual such as Shamanism and Native American philosophy with the author's own education to help individuals prepare for this time of awakening. IlgaAnn Bunjer is a true teacher and has opened my heart to the amazing way that science truly is a bridge to spirituality."

Kimmie Rose Zapf
Author of Wake Up Your Intuition, CBS radio host,
Inner views With Kimmie and Steve

DEDICATION

This book is dedicated to all the light workers on planet Earth, along with those looking for answers about the Universe and their place in it. It is also a tangible thank-you to the Creator for the peace and joy in my heart and to all that exists in the great Circle of Life.

ACKNOWLEDGMENTS

Before I acknowledge anyone, I want to make it clear that the information in this book came from my heart, memories, and spirit guidance. I am 100 percent Latvian in this lifetime. I do not intend to steal the spirituality that belongs to the Native Americans and should be honored as their cultural belief system. There is much misinformation being given out, and many individuals are trying to capitalize on native spirituality as a way of making a buck. I do not think such exploitation is ethical.

However, I have been guided and given information. My spirit guides keep telling me to share some concepts of ancient wisdom so that everyone can understand how all of us are part of the Circle of Life. In this book I will blend beliefs from several different cultures, including Native American cultures, with science and psychology. The design of the book is to educate by explaining separate origin and historical concepts to create awareness and a desire for further exploration of those ideas. The intention is education and spiritual enlightenment as we build the bridge to a new and better world.

I want to thank the Great Spirit/God/Creator and all my guides and helpers—both physical and spiritual—who have helped me in the process of writing. They have opened my eyes and my heart to a whole new world and future. Most of all I thank my patient and supportive husband, Kirk, for his continued love and tolerance of late meals (if he got fed at all), along with other signs of neglect. Your input and commitment to helping me with this task was of great value. I could not have done it without your able assistance and confidence. I also want to acknowledge the support of all my friends and other family members. I apologize for my inattentiveness to you while I concentrated on this book.

Another sincere appreciation goes to one of my dearest friends and experienced editor, Kathy Johansen, who worked so diligently to make sure what I had written made sense to those not familiar with New Age philosophy and terms. My gratitude overflows for your efforts.

In addition to my family and friends, I also want to acknowledge the wonderful support and help from all the terrific staff of my publisher.

Finally, a great big hug of appreciation goes to you, the reader, for your interest and desire to raise your consciousness and reconnect to the Creator.

Thank you all from the bottom of my heart.

Mitakuye Oyasin (We are all related).

—IlgaAnn

CONTENTS

INTRODUCTION

*We shall require a substantially new manner of thinking
if mankind is to survive.*

—Albert Einstein

The human race has always wondered where it is from, where it's going, and what its purpose is. This book will answer those questions. In addition it will show how humankind is part of a reemerging Star Nation and more.

The purpose of this book is to offer information about how things work in the Universe as it reminds us of the ancient indigenous ways of living in balance and harmony with all that exists in creation, or *All That Is*.

Some of the information may seem contrary to what many have been taught to believe. You may want to consider what is offered in this book as alternative truths. One's perspective on life is the most highly personal aspect of perception. Please take what you want and leave the rest.

This is not a channeled book, where everything comes directly from a nonphysical entity(s). A large portion of the information in this book comes from years of personal communications with spirit guides. I work with many different spirit messengers, some of which are animals. My primary spirit guide is Heyoak, a Hopi clown in a former life. But I also work with a wolf, bear, eagle, spider, and raven, among others. I get messages from varied resources, including the Universal Star Council of Light, to whom I will credit most of the direct quotes.

Ancient Spirit Wisdom: An Elder's Guidebook To Native Spirituality and Beyond materialized through the challenging work of interpreting personal dreams and visions by asking questions and by receiving psychically intuitive knowledge. Additional information is the result of research and consultation with and input from others, including psychics and medicine people.

In today's world there are several explanations of how individuals might access information in nonordinary ways. Many healers have suggested that all humans have the ability to be psychic—if they open their minds to possibilities and suspend conventional belief systems. Some are born with their psychic capabilities fully functional. For others, there are schools and books designed to help develop and enhance innate psychic abilities.

Scholarly explanations of human psychic ability are generally based on what Jungian or analytic psychologies call the *collective unconscious*. Carl Jung, the originator of what came to be known as the school of Jungian psychology, was one of Sigmund Freud's students and contemporaries. Both Jung and Freud were advocates of a collective unconscious that can be accessed.

The concept of a collective unconscious seems to be a universal cultural phenomenon. Some cultures know it as nonordinary reality. Deepak Chopra calls it *the invisible intelligence*. One can say that in many cultures, healers, shamans, or medicine men and women use wisdom of the collective unconscious.

Shamanism is an ancient spiritual practice dating back 30,000 to 40,000 years and originating in Russia's Ural Mountains. Shamanism is not a Native American practice, although that is how it is often presented in New Age literature. The term *shaman* has come to represent any individual who works with nonordinary reality. In the past, virtually all the indigenous tribes had a shaman-type healer or medicine man. This person could contact the unseen world by altering his state of consciousness and taking a shamanic or soul journey. While on this journey, the shaman communicated with spirits, who shared information or helped with healing.

Today, persons undergoing nontraditional hypnosis may access alternate realities in time, space, and location. Many books have been written concerting such experiences using this technique. One well-known book of this genre is *Many Lives, Many Masters* by Brian L. Weiss.

When we spend time meditating or listening to the silence within our subconscious, we may eventually begin to access information from nonordinary reality. This process has been assigned various labels, including being psychic, having intuitive knowledge, or channeling.

On a daily basis we gather ordinary information through the use of our senses—sight, hearing, touch, smell, and taste. But those same senses can also access nonordinary reality through the use of our intuitive abilities. Everyone has what we call the "sixth sense," our intuition, or "gut feeling." The following are the most common terms applied to the use of the sixth sense in accessing nonordinary reality:

1. Clairvoyance through vision, otherwise called clear seeing.
2. Clairaudience through clear hearing.
3. Clairsentience through clear touch.
4. Clairalience through smelling something not really present, clear smelling.

5. Clairambience through clear taste of something not there but representing nonphysical matter, energy, or spirit presence.

These are all channels of information referred to as extrasensory perception or ESP. People are often frightened by this message and shut down their abilities while others work on enhancing these skills. Traditional religion frowns on ESP abilities and claim that they come from an evil influence. More information on this topic can be found in chapter 12, "Earth-Bound Spirits, Lost Souls, and the Astral Plane."

The spirit guides tell me,

> *A vision originates from a person's own spiritual energy within. The process of seeing the vision serves as a bridge to cross the gap between the physical and the spiritual worlds. The vision creates an alignment of these two aspects. If within the vision you are given directions on how to produce something (e.g., a book, a staff, or other object) it is important to work on manifesting whatever was seen in the vision.*

We are living in a time of change, violence, chaos, and confusion—environmentally, politically, personally, and energetically. Many individuals, especially the youth, have lost their sense of identity and purpose. Many are existing on just a day-to-day basis. Youth are joining gangs to feel a sense of belonging and safety. Others are using drugs to help them cope with life or to escape an unpleasant reality. Humanity is experiencing an increasing number of wars, conflicts, earthquakes, and storms. Fires rage across drought-stricken land; volcanoes hurl molten lava; hurricanes, high winds, and tornadoes are becoming more frequent and more destructive. All of these factors combine to cause significant Earth changes.

A whole new spiritually based lifestyle movement called the New Age has been rapidly growing in popularity. Based on lifestyle change, the New Age is sometimes referred to as the shift of consciousness or simply *the Shift* because of the major changes that are taking place on the planet and within its residents.

As individuals evolve to higher spiritual consciousness, they become more aware that something is wrong, and they begin searching for solutions. Based on the questions and comments we get from attendees of the metaphysical/whole health fairs where I display my gems and minerals, many feel a growing sense of urgency and are desperately looking for the truth. Many seem to want to know how to make a deeper spiritual connection to fill the void within themselves. Others are writing books about their experiences and sharing new research and insights about the realities of our world and about life after death. However, more information is still needed. The Universe and how it all fits together is a mystery. All our efforts are just scratching the surface of what there is to know and understand—wisdom once held by the ancient civilizations. Some of that information is beginning to surface again as we move toward the Shift.

So Why Write A Book?

I keep receiving consistent messages through dreams and intuition; they direct me to write this book so others can also benefit from the knowledge I have been receiving. Recently I was told by a Native American psychic's spirit guide, "Wisdom not shared is equivalent to being a horse thief, because you are depriving others of something they need." Spirit can certainly motivate a person with a sense of humor to help get our attention and make a point.

My guides tell me I need to share my insights with others as part of my prebirth life contract. My life purpose contract tells me I am in this world not only to learn personal lessons but also to be a messenger, teacher, and healer. I am to serve as a bridge builder between the spiritual and human dimensions. (See chapter 2, "Humankind's Purpose and Life Contract Lessons.")

When meditating or writing I sense the energy of the Sacred Circle of Light around me, and I tap into it for help and protection from the negative energies of the world. The Sacred Circle is representative of the Sacred Hoop of Life or the medicine wheel spoken about by Black Elk in *Black Elk Speaks* by John G. Neihardt. If I close my eyes, I can see the Circle of Light around me. I feel its energy vibration, which emits a very warm, loving, and comfortable feeling of balance and harmony. It is with these wonderful feelings that I begin this journey.

I'm writing to share information and to help humanity understand that there is much more to life than we realize. The flow of this book's design starts with mankind's focus and purpose and then defines the spiritual source of the book's information in part 1, "Belief Systems."

Part 2, "The Beginning," moves on to explain our connection to the Star Nation of the Native American culture and how our body has a built-in connection to the stars.

Part 3, "Dimensions of Existence," continues to clarify how things work in our lives.

Part 4, "Action Steps for Your Life Journey," concludes by giving information and tools for personal soul growth.

This publication is designed to be a guidebook so humans can reconnect to the spiritual flame in their hearts and re-experience the interconnected community of all things—the Oneness. Those who are already connected to Spirit know that their souls are light energy. These are the light workers helping a sleeping humanity wake up to their higher consciousness.

PART 1

Belief Systems

CHAPTER 1

Guidance

Pay attention to your dreams—God's angels often speak directly to our hearts when we are asleep.
—Eileen Elias Freeman, *The Angels' Instruction Book*

As I type the words of this book, I perceive what seems to be a thought message but what is really intuitive guidance concerning what needs to be said—not specific words, just ideas. As a general rule I feel warm waves of positive energy washing over me rather than physically seeing or hearing my guides. When they do appear, the Universal Star Council of Light members are tall, misty, semi-translucent fields of light with no gender designations. They leave me comforted with a sense of peace, joy, and respect. I do not feel judged or criticized, because they represent unconditional love. I receive visions and sometimes intuitive knowledge about the meaning of the vision.

What Is Your Purpose, Universal Star Council of Light?

We call ourselves the Council of Light Beings. We are "light keepers," but there is not a word in your language that truly

describes us. A Council of Light is the closest we can come
to give you some understanding of our nature. We are not
physical beings. We are pure spirit, or what you call light
energy/consciousness. Ours is a world of energy—a spirit
world that exists as an interconnected web. We refer to this
place as the Oneness. We are not the Creator, but we are
a part of Him.

To help the reader understand the concept of the interconnected web of the Oneness, the best visual example comes from the *Star Trek* television series. One of the characters in this series was called Odo. He was a shape-shifter; he could change his complete physical appearance to anything else he chose. Odo's home, his planet of origin, was a large ocean consisting of a multitude of others like himself. Upon returning "home," he would walk in and *meld* back into the ocean, becoming like an individual drop of the ocean, aware of itself but also a part of the whole. This is the interconnectedness to everything in existence that I mentioned in this book's introduction and how the Oneness functions.

The Council continues,

The Akashic Records, ethereal records of all actions, thoughts,
and feelings which have occurred or will ever occur, are kept
where we are. We are the "Voice" spoken of in the Christian
Bible [Revelation 16:1.] *We are where you originally came*
from. As the voice of Spirit we want to help humanity find
the forgotten "Jewel," the spiritual connection to its soul.
Our role is to help guide humans and to remind them
who they are and where they are from. We help humanity
know what its life purpose is. Our role is to foster the well-

being and spiritual growth of mankind. We teach about meditation, spiritual awakening, and understanding. We are not here to give humanity directions, just guidance.

Our task as a Council is to be the vision and light keepers. That means we hold the vision of the Universe. The earth does not have any light of its own. The light that represents understanding, wisdom, and truth comes from the sun, the moon, and the stars. That is the only way light illuminates the earth. Light is vision. You cannot see without it. Without light, the earth is a dark, bottomless pit. Humankind needs to reestablish a relationship with the stars and reconnect to the light in order for physical life to continue on Earth.

We are not channeled. We bring our message as we come into ceremony or the energy of the Sacred Circle. True medicine people can hear us. We are communicating with you to teach the ways of the ancient ancestors—how to live in balance and harmony with life. When we speak of "ancient," it is from a point when time began. We want humanity to understand and be more awake. That is why it is important for you to develop your own spiritual connection to the Oneness.

A Message of Reinforcement

I had a recent dream reinforcing the need for humankind to wake up because many are unaware. In essence, they are sleeping and have forgotten how to connect to Spirit. But people don't know they've forgotten how to connect, so they have to be reminded. Here is my recollection of that dream:

I was lying on the ground in front of a big government building. Lots of men and women were lying around me. They had their eyes shut as if they were asleep. I noticed a big brown and beige tom turkey walking among all the scattered bodies on the ground. Every now and then the turkey would stop and start pecking at someone's eyes. This frightened me, as I imagined the pain and destruction his beak could inflict on my ability to see. Then the turkey came over and stopped by me. I froze in fear, afraid for the safety of my eyes. Instead of pecking at my eyes, he said, "Get up! You are not asleep like these others. You need to write and teach them to wake up."

A Prophetic Dream

My other spirit guides often send me prophetic dreams. I recently experienced what seems to be an important one. The dream included five birds: the eagle, the crow, the raven, the owl, and the hawk. They were flying side by side, equidistant to each other as though in formation. They flew past me and landed on the ground close by, still in formation.

When I asked for clarity on the meaning of the dream, the Universal Star Council of Light responded with the following information:

> *The five birds represent the five energetic pathways. These pathways go in two directions, from the human world to the spirit dimension and back again. Spirit also travels both ways. The dream came to you because you are working on this book, which will create a bridge between the worlds— the physical and the spiritual dimensions.*
>
> *You are helping to build the bridge, and all similar bridges being built in different parts of the world by different*

people, when put together, will create a Spiritual Ark. The
energy of the Ark is light, but its message is about trusting
and acting on faith while living a spiritually aware life to
prepare for the new world of balance and harmony.

The Spiritual Ark is similar to the physical ark built by Noah (Genesis 6:14–22 KJV) to save his family and representatives of all of Earth's other living creatures from being destroyed by the flood. For additional information about the Spiritual Ark, read the *Hopi Survival Kit* by Thomas Mails.

An Interpretation

It is important to understand the day-to-day application and meaning of the dream these winged pathway messengers carry. When we understand the dream's message, we can choose to listen to the guidance and live our lives appropriately. Here is what the birds symbolize, according to the Universal Star Council of Light:

The eagle represents a vision of peace and hope. The eagle travels
through many dimensions in taking your prayers to the Great
Mystery (God). The dimensions through which he travels represent
a pathway between our physical world and the world of spirit.
The process of receiving and giving information is what creates the
bridge between these dimensions. This is spiritual law.

The crow stands for spiritual law. The crow's pathway
represents the need for humans to learn about and share
the knowledge of spiritual laws. This is what is meant by
the pathway going in two directions. [What spiritual laws

are and what they mean will be discussed in chapter 4, "Universal Codes of Life."]

The raven is the magical pathway of faith. Have faith and become more comfortable with the Great Mystery, which is not really hidden. The mystery is revealed as you go forward and practice faith. [Hebrews 11:1 defines faith as "the substance of things hoped for, the evidence of things not seen."]

The owl is symbolic of different things in different cultures. It has been known as the bird of wisdom because it is awake at night and because it can turn its head so far around. An owl is the spirit bird—the spirit watcher. It represents the transition from one world to another. The owl is the transition pathway from the physical world to the spiritual world. This is what the Shift means. In the past when the owl was heard, it signified death. Today this same sound signifies a shift of consciousness. This can be thought of as the death of the old world and the subsequent transformation of the awakening of spiritual consciousness, which is also known as the Shift.

The hawk has clear, sharp, detailed observation. Hawks represent the pathway of teaching and the quality of being observant. The hawk signals you to pay attention to what is going on. As you cross the bridge you must learn the details you will need to know so you can take the appropriate steps to correct your own actions or to help others. Hawks also represent bridging but in a different way than the crow's spiritual bridge to the physical world. With hawks, knowing the details is essential.

Modern mankind has forgotten the significance of the messages revealed in this dream. Such messages are being retold to anyone who will listen and receive. These messages will continue to come from dreams. They will come in visions; they will come from the animals; and they will come from your own personal spirit guides. They may even come through other persons with whom you interact. You must open your heart to receive these spirit messages, which are timely, important pieces of information. The buffalo has already gone forth. The path is here, the spiritual path.

This is a summary of the dream's meaning. Humanity needs to hold a vision of hope and peace in the world. They need to learn the spiritual laws, practice them, and then teach the laws to others in our life as part of our personal soul growth and life purpose. Have faith in the desired outcome. This will help the world and humanity have a successful shift of consciousness to a higher level. We must pay attention to what is going on and take the necessary steps to correct our own actions as we walk the spiritual path.

The Council states,

At this time in the world, there is a war present within many different countries, but the war is also internal in human beings. The conflict is happening within human consciousness, the war between the light and the dark energies. The voice of light speaks the truth, but the voice of darkness also has a presence that speaks within individuals and situations. What you choose within your life will allow you to go forward and help others. Pay attention. Trust and follow the visions, dreams, and messages that have come to you. These messages are very important, so take them very seriously. There is a reason and a purpose why you have received this information. Through your actions you will show if you are following the information and walking the Red Road or not.

Walking the Native American Red Road, the road of spirituality, is similar to living by the Golden Rule noted in the Christian Bible. If you choose to walk the Red Road, blessings and help from the Spirit will accompany you. If you choose not to walk this road, then difficulties and interference will accompany you. This is not a threat; it is part of the Spiritual Law, which says that you attract what you focus on.

Everything has increased in speed. You need to open your heart so that the creative energy can move through your human body. In terms of changes that are taking place, there is a need for communities of people to gather and listen to each other, to pray and reconnect with ceremonies to bring spiritual energy into this plane. This is what has been prophesied.

Other Messengers

The buffalo has also brought a message. The message is a vision of peace and harmony within this world. The buffalo represents the world, as well as our human connection to the natural world all around us. All of life's building blocks and elements present in the world are also present in the buffalo. From ancient times the Native Americans have called this the spiritual path of the buffalo the Red Road. This is the road of spirituality, harmony, and recognition of our interconnected relationship with all that exists in the material world. The Sioux tribes refer to this interconnection as *All My Relations*, signifying that our actions affect and are related to the earth and everything that exists on it.

Our total interconnection with everything in existence is a significant ideological concept to accept. The best modern way of explaining our universal interconnection is exemplified by the butterfly effect from the chaos theory. The butterfly effect tells us that any small event in one part of the world can have a major impact somewhere else, far away. For example, a butterfly wing's flutter in Italy could impact the atmosphere in such a way that it causes changes that create a storm in Canada.

My college physics class had a technical term for this effect—the sensitive dependence on initial conditions. My social work therapy class called it the *mobile effect*; if one part of a hanging mobile is touched, the other parts move as well. These models show how ancient wisdom gets changed and rephrased from a new scientific perspective. But it still means we have a connection to each other and everything in our world, even if we do not perceive it that way.

The indigenous peoples applied the concept of interconnection on a global level to create balance and harmony. How they treated each other and the earth is one example of the daily application of this concept. Everything was done with the idea in mind that seven generations past, the ancestors were looking down from above and watching the people's actions. In addition, the next seven generations yet to be born were considered as looking up from the earth. Consequently, things had to be done in a way to not offend either group of observers.

For instance, when collecting herbs for healing or food, in consideration of others' needs, the collector always asked for permission from the plant to take a portion. After intuitively gaining permission, they never took more than they needed and used all they took. There was an unspoken rule to never take more than one third from any particular plant. In this way, there was always some left for others and for the plant to keep growing for use at another time. Many herbalists still practice this rule when harvesting in nature.

A Wake-Up Call!

Spirit has a way of reminding us of what we are here to do if we pay attention to our dreams and our intuitive gut feelings. The dreams that stay in our memories or are consistently being repeated are messages from your higher-self and your spirit guides. Pay attention and try to understand what you are being told. Keeping a dream diary is helpful and a good idea.

CHAPTER 2

Humankind's Purpose and Life Contract Lessons

I know God will not give me anything I can't handle. I just wish He didn't trust me so much.

—Mother Theresa

Spirit says,

> *Human beings are basically a light consciousness that has evolved from Spirit. This is the purpose for which Earth was created, to give souls a place to make the choice between light consciousness and the negative shadow side, otherwise known as the dark side.*

> *At the beginning of time, the Oneness had a plan for this planet. All the different beings from other places were given*

a certain amount of time to accomplish that purpose. That time is almost up.

From the Council's perspective,

Atlantean and Egyptian times are recent.

The Mayans, Hopi, Cherokee, and many others call this present time the Fourth Cycle, the time of purification. It is projected in the Mayan calendar that this cycle will close on December 21, 2012. At that time, humanity is supposed to enter into the Fifth Cycle, which will be the one of peace and harmony

Over the millennia, humanity became distanced from the Star Nation of the Universe and the original purpose. The ancient civilizations still had the connection to Spirit. But at present, humanity has lost that connection. Humanity needs to wake up and renew that spiritual connection. Essentially, human beings today are like children attending school again, with varied subject lessons to learn in each new grade. As we evolve spiritually, we pass on to a higher grade or level of consciousness. Each level of existence has its own purpose and lessons to be learned. The teachers who have come to help at this time are the angels. However, many old souls who were alive on the legendary sunken continent of Atlantis, where they still had the spiritual connection, have also reincarnated to help humankind evolve.

Before we are born, our souls know what our spiritual growth needs are before we can reach a higher plane of conscious evolution. The soul then develops a plan, a personal life contract designed to expose us to life situations where we can learn those lessons and achieve optimum spiritual growth. At times our lives' roles might only be to serve as examples, good or bad, so that others can learn by observing our actions. However, humans always have free will to choose whether to fulfill the soul's original plan or not.

Based on Spirit's guidance, the following is the overall lesson plan for humankind—our life purpose. There are four common goals and varied levels of choice and commitment.

Level One—General and Personal Purpose

General Purpose Tasks

The general purpose tasks that everyone needs to work on accomplishing are

- cultivating personal spirituality by waking up and reconnecting to Spirit;
- learning the Spiritual Laws and living by them daily;
- maintaining a positive attitude in life;
- learning to care for our bodies in a healthy way;
- learning to live in balance and harmony with everything around us—other people, animals, the land, trees, flowers, water, etc.;
- overcoming our fears and doubts, regardless of what our life situations may be.

These are not always easy tasks to accomplish and often take much perseverance and help.

Personal Purpose Tasks

In addition to the general tasks, each person has a personal purpose, with individual, specific variations on the general tasks. This personal purpose consists of private spiritual growth and expression, including the soul lessons that apply to one's own life situations. It is necessary to work on all the areas listed at the same time.

For example, in addition to all the general tasks, your personal life contract could be to develop a positive attitude regardless of what obstacles and problems you are facing. The problems encountered offer situations where you can learn and grow spiritually as each lesson is completed. As hard as it might seem, always be grateful for the potholes of life because these obstacles become opportunities to discover what you need to do differently.

It appears that the Universe and our guides are persistent in helping us learn. If a lesson is not learned from a particular situation, that lesson keeps repeating with other varied but similar formats. It has been my observation that often the situations also keep escalating in seriousness until we do something different to resolve it or until everything falls apart, including your body. I've observed that humans often need the emotional equivalent of a two-by-four to the head to come to a realization that what they are doing is not working. It is common to get physically ill from problem-related worry and stress from the decreased effectiveness of the immune system.

Helen's Lesson Story

Helen (not her real name) is a good example of a lesson that kept repeating itself. Helen needed to learn to value and speak up for herself. She had been born into a family where she did not receive the love, approval, and nurturance she needed to learn self-worth. To escape an unhappy home life, she married a man who was critical, cold, and distant, not unlike the environment she had become familiar with in her childhood. After divorcing her first husband, she married a man who was addicted to alcohol and work. This was another man who was not emotionally available to give her what she needed. The players varied, but the situations were the same.

In relationships it is common for persons to consistently pick the same type of individual and set up circumstances to continue receiving the same learning opportunity.

Now, many years later, Helen is realizing that she is not happy with the way things are and that she has to change her perspective on things. Helen realizes she has to set limits/boundaries on how she allows herself to be treated and not believe that another's shortcomings automatically create inevitable consequences for her to accept and live with.

The life lesson of self-respect from her personal purpose contract has finally started to sink in. However, it has taken many years of heartbreak and health problems. The lesson is not complete yet; awareness is only the first step. The next step is remembering to change her reactions, thoughts, and behaviors on a daily basis. It is very easy to backslide into old habits. Through these relationships, Helen is learning to value her own needs and to speak up for them. Helen's parents and husbands were doing their part in setting up circumstances for her to learn while at the same time fulfilling their own life contract agreements to serve as teachers.

Universal Laws of Attraction

If during difficult times you tend to focus your thoughts on worrying about the problem instead of looking for possible solutions, you could get more of the same problem you are worrying about to begin with. Remember, whatever you focus on, you get more of, whether the consequences are positive or negative. This is the Universal Law of Attraction, a Spiritual Law. Energy follows thought, so we create more of whatever we think about. When we feel resentment or anger, focusing on it only makes it grow in intensity. Inadvertently we often become our own worst enemies.

In the middle of a negative thought, feeling, or situation, stop and ask yourself, "Is this thought helping or hindering my spiritual, mental, or physical progress?" If it is not, change it. You can pray, meditate, or ask your guides to help you.

A popular book, CD, and DVD titled *The Secret* by Rhonda Byrne explores the concept of the Universal Law of Attraction and how we get what we focus on. Linda's story illustrates how learning to focus on the positive attracted positive elements into her life.

During my practice as a therapist and life coach, I have encountered a number of clients who were stuck in a specific pothole of life and needed help climbing out. Linda's story is one example.

Linda's Story

Linda (not her real name) was an attractive and talented young woman who was experiencing a difficult life. She was struggling with alcoholism, had been a victim of domestic violence, and suffered from low self-esteem. Her life seemed to keep getting worse. She was miserable and did not know what to do. Spirit often keeps raising the difficulty of a situation until we finally pay attention.

Then Linda was in an auto accident. In the hospital emergency room, she died but made the choice to come back.

Eventually Linda recognized that she needed to change her life. With that positive thought in her mind, people she met—strangers— stepped up to help her. She kept a positive outlook but also made a plan of action and followed through with it. Even in the face of pain, she persevered in getting her life back to a better place, a place where she wanted and needed to be. Linda is still working on reprogramming her thought patterns to learn her life lessons and is making great progress.

Through her suffering, Linda learned that certain aspects of her life needed to be changed, and that revelation constituted her personal spiritual growth. Linda's experience has also given others the opportunity to help her.

Those who helped Linda in her recovery were fulfilling their life contract lessons by being of service to others while doing their own spiritual growth on levels one and two. This story also demonstrates how we interconnect with each other through our relationships.

Helping Others

In addition to personal growth, another part of your personal purpose might be to use your innate abilities to benefit others. It could be that you are to become a healer through the use of your talents. Maybe you can sing, dance, write, teach or have some other special skill or talent (e.g., plumbing, farming, carpentry, playing sports), and as you use that talent or skill, others are helped or entertained. Everything we do or don't do has a ripple effect on everything around us.

There is one important thing to keep in mind as you learn and grow spiritually: the more you exercise opening your heart; expressing compassion, love, and patience; and learning those lessons that you are here to learn, the brighter your spiritual flame becomes. If you choose greed and selfishness, you are only serving your own desires, and the spiritual flame diminishes.

Level Two—Friends and Family Purpose

The first extensions of level-one lessons are to all of your friends and family. Share with your friends and family the lessons you have learned and the practice of a level-one lifestyle. Level two is about being a role model and teacher.

However, friends and family always have the choice of free will of whether or not to accept this lifestyle. If your friends and family choose to reject your lifestyle, do not blame yourself. No one is responsible for choices made by others. All you can do is present the information, plant the seed of awareness. Level two is about accepting the responsibility to serve as a model and teacher without forcing or demanding that others comply.

In Linda's case, a role model she used was one of the authors of *90 Minutes in Heaven,* Don Piper and Cecil Murphey. Don Piper's description of his ongoing experience with pain helped Linda cope with her own suffering.

Being a role model or teacher is an important assignment. Parents, teachers, ministers, friends, and even politicians model behaviors and teach us how to act to be accepted and fit into the culture we live in. Some of the examples they set and lessons they teach are good while others show negative behavior and leave a lot to be desired. Corporations spend millions of dollars on advertising to convince us of what we need in our lives. Such advertising is not true role modeling, but it does create a sample lifestyle we often strive to duplicate, which can distract us from the spiritual path.

Some of the daily information we are bombarded with is helpful, but often it does not serve to help us in our spiritual growth. I have heard ministers quote the Bible and tell us to "be in this world but not of it." In the past, this phrase always confused me, but now its meaning is clear. Humanity is not native to Earth but here to learn and grow and reconnect to Spirit. To be spiritual and walk the path of a light worker does not always fit the materialistic and violent world we live in. When facing a difficult situation, ask yourself, "How would Mother Theresa or the Dalai Lama behave under the same circumstances?" There are many good spiritual role models. Who are yours?

Level Three—Global Purpose

The second extensions of the level-one lessons are on a global effort, teaching groups of people for world-scale evolution. The task is to recognize the needs of the larger family of all mankind. We help the world and the Universe as a whole by working on a global level.

Level three is the way of the Native American Sacred Hoop and the Sacred Circle of Life, where everything is considered interrelated. The Sioux Nation has a term that sums it all up—*Mitakuye Oyasin*, meaning *we are all related* or, as they say it, *All My Relations*. This term represents humankind's interconnection with all animate and inanimate life in creation.

Everything carries its own energy and vibration. It encompasses humans, animals (the two-legged, the four-legged, the winged ones, and those who swim and crawl), rocks, trees, elements, and the planet itself. Indigenous peoples respect and honor all creation without feeling the need to own or control it. The path of truth, the Red Road, occurs when one walks with spirit, obeying the Universal Codes of Life (discussed chapter 4). It is important to learn about the Universal Laws while still in the physical realm.

Level-three lessons incorporate a larger scale, but for this level to be completed there must be a manifested product outcome. The product outcome could be a book, song, a workshop, a new type of business style, or any number of other possibilities. However, it must represent something tangible that can be shared with others.

The book Linda found so helpful, *90 Minutes in Heaven*, this book is an example of a tangible product based on one's experience that others can benefit from. This book is another example.

Level Four—Master Teacher Purpose

The angels and master souls visiting Earth at this time also have a purpose. They have come here to help. Their purpose is to be the master teachers of humanity. They appear as earthly teachers who have been sent to help the world make a major change and complete the Shift mentioned in this book's introduction. Individuals who need to make personal changes seek out these teachers. New Age author and lecturer Doreen Virtue describes how to recognize these "angels" and other special helpers in her books, *Earth Angels* and *Realms of Earth Angels*.

One purpose is not better or worse than another; they are just different. Purpose levels and lessons are not to be judged. Doing global work does not mean that your personal growth will be greater than someone who is working on a level-one purpose. Those who have contracted to do global work still need to do individual and family/friends work as well. If you do not do levels one and level two, then you are deluding yourself in your ability to do global work. Effectiveness on each level depends on your ability to open yourself to and to bring forth universal energy. As you practice level one—individual work—you become more and more skilled in bringing forth energy. Level two—friends and family work—prepares you to teach larger audiences. It all fits together, making it important to work on the first three levels at all times.

The Spiritual Life Contract

Everyone has a spiritual life purpose contract, although you probably do not remember signing it before you were born. This contract is between your soul, or higher-self as some call it, and the Creator. The life lessons you selected for yourself will help you learn a higher perspective so your soul can grow spiritually. Those lessons will keep coming back in different ways until you have learned them, as Helen's story demonstrates. Many individuals have forgotten all about this contract that specifies why you were born the way you are and what you need to accomplish in this lifetime.

My Life Purpose Contract

The life contract can be long and complicated with many details, depending on each person's soul needs. For example, my personal life contract, in part, designates that I am here to learn patience, independence, compassion, and trusting what I know to be true, among other lessons. In addition, I am also here to be a messenger, teacher, healer, and builder of bridges between the material and spirit worlds.

I continue to do my personal growth work daily, remembering Spiritual Law and what I'm here to learn. The interaction with my friends, family, and clients represent level-two work. The presentations, workshops, and written materials are all part of my global tasks.

The reason I lived through World War II and other life obstacles has been to learn that I can survive and can teach coping skills to others on both the friends and family level plus a global scale. I was born with specific latent skills and talents to help me accomplish the necessary tasks. In addition, there have been many physical teachers along my life-path who have guided and instructed me. Chapter 21, "How Spirit Has Guided My Life," delves further into some of my history to give you some insights.

There are multiple ways to fulfill your life purpose contract. For example, if you did not learn something as a child like you had planned, you can learn it later even in the final few years of your earthly life. However, during your lifetime you always have free will to choose whether to fulfill the contract or omit certain parts. The consequence is that when your life ends and there are lessons still left undone, you will have to come back in another lifetime and complete them. Ultimately every lesson must be learned. You cannot skip any of them.

Everyone has personal work to do as part of a process toward perfection and returning to the source of our origin. Spiritual growth is a process. In essence, everyone needs to work on the first three purpose levels continuously: personal growth, friends and family teaching/role modeling, and sharing wisdom on a global level so others can benefit.

As you work on each level of tasks, you need to keep the expected outcome clearly in mind. For example, you are presenting a workshop about domestic violence prevention, and a large audience from many places has come to hear the presentation. If you perceive that you are using your personal skills in helping each participant within that group, then you are doing personal level work with a level-one vibration. However, if you see it intended as global work and helping the world by giving the group new information, then the presentation will carry the global energy vibration.

Keep in mind that the scope of tasks necessary for each level of purpose are varied based on what is effective in reaching the appropriate audience. For example, the concept of growth on a personal level versus family/friends level is different and changes again for the global level.

On a personal level, growth, in part, could include

- learning and practicing spiritual laws;
- keeping a positive attitude toward life;
- doing meditation;
- prayer;
- exercise;
- volunteering to help those in need;
- not abusing your body through food, alcohol, or anything else.

On a friends/family level, growth could include

- sharing your personal growth knowledge and experience;
- helping those in your life understand what's damaging to the body;
- role modeling behaviors.

While on a global level, growth might include

- writing articles about what you have learned to spread that information;
- starting a petition to ban something damaging to the environment.

A partial interpretation of *giving* on each of the levels might include the following:

- Level one—volunteer your time, money, and/or talents without expecting anything in return, even if this means personal sacrifice. Give freely, as in random acts of kindness.
- Level two—giving examples could be taking in a sibling's children when the sibling is not able to care for them. Again, this involves stepping in and taking over because it is the right thing to do, without expecting anything back.
- Level three—at this level, an example of giving could be setting up a foundation designed to serve others. The USO volunteer entertainment group traveling into war zones to lift the morale of the military is another example.

Spirit advises,

> *There should always be a balance of energy exchanged in all manner of giving and receiving, regardless of whether*

the giving consists of tangible items or through the provision of emotional support for another person. An imbalance of energy develops if the receiver of the gift does not appreciate it, takes it for granted, or discounts it. For example, you consistently forgive another's misbehavior without trying to correct it, or you keep giving material items like jewelry or flowers but they are not valued. Giving endlessly when it is not appreciated and reciprocated is like putting the gift into a dark hole with a mirror in the bottom of the hole. As the positive energy of the gift hits the mirror on the bottom, it reverses direction to counterclockwise and comes back to you as a negative energy.

Regardless of which level you are working on, do not give your gifts if they are not properly received. As Jesus was purported to have stated, "Cast not pearls before swine." Spirit advises that it is not good to waste your resources in that manner. The lesson in this exchange then becomes one of setting boundaries on when and to whom you give.

Reading the Life Contract

You can achieve the ability to understand your life contract by working on the three life purpose levels. In addition you can call upon your angels or spirit guides to help you grow and interpret the contract.

As you evolve spiritually toward the light consciousness, you will intuitively be attracted to certain tasks, choices, jobs, behaviors, and people. On the other hand, if you are not evolving with the light consciousness, you will lean toward the negative shadow side tasks, behaviors, and people. Everything is on a vibratory level, and that is why it is so important to work on all three purpose levels simultaneously to raise your vibration and consciousness level as you grow and evolve spiritually.

Spirit explains,

> *Your soul/higher-self is operating from the imprint of the life purpose lessons that you agreed to before your birth, as recorded in the life contract. Your intuition will guide you to its general contents. However, for the purpose to be fully known and understood, your spiritual growth level must have evolved to the point where you can receive and interpret the contract. The agreement is "written" on both a cellular level and a light vibratory level. Verbal explanations of the contract do not make sense because there are no words for energetic meaning.*

> *In order for a person's consciousness to evolve to the point of being able to read the contract, it needs to match the vibration level of the soul at its highest rate. Reading the contract is like reading a crystal; you have to have the ability to understand the informational imprint. If you cannot read it, then you cannot fulfill it. So you will have to come back in another lifetime for more growth until you have raised your consciousness vibration rate and the life purpose can be fulfilled. Working on the three life purpose levels is how you achieve this ability.*

All your chakras (energy centers) need to be open, and your own energy has to be in the higher vibratory level. Not everyone has the ability to hold the light and energy necessary to read his or her contract. However, there are individuals whose life tasks include helping others read their contracts. This is where faith and trust come in to know that the information is available and accurate from true light workers.

There are many individuals who agreed to fulfill their contracts; however, once in physical form, they have chosen not to accomplish their life purposes. Some chose not to honor the contract because they felt that there was too much personal sacrifice involved; others got distracted through addiction or greed. Many think that their success is contingent on their life's material possessions or their bank accounts. Big mistake! Your spiritual evolution depends on the actions you choose to take after your birth. Individuals become lost by focusing on the material world and being comfortable, so they never learn about sacrifice or true giving. They will have to repeat life after life until they learn and understand what it means to be interconnected, to become nurturing and respectful of all living things.

A Wake-Up Call!

The Light Council says,

> *What you do in this lifetime, which is a gift from the Creator, will determine your future. What you choose to do today will contribute to the true future of planet Earth. How you live your life is important. In choosing the light, you do things that nourish the mind, body, and heart instead of choosing those things that create illness and weakness within the physical body.*

CHAPTER 3

Religion

This is my simple religion. There is no need for temples; no need for complicated philosophy. Our own brain, our own heart is our temple; the philosophy is kindness.

—Dalai Lama

The Council states,

> *The information we are giving you for this book is the Living Word, and as people read it, they will feel the vibration of the words. The Living Word is the vibration of light consciousness translated into speech.* ***The words carry an energy frequency, which is the language of life put into words.***

> *As this book is read, the impact of the information will be assimilated on both physical and mental levels. This action*

will help humanity wake up to a deeper and more complex
vision of the Universe.

An example of how human words and thoughts can impact the molecules of water illustrates the above statement from Spirit. The human body consists of a minimum of 70 percent water, which is an excellent conductor of electricity. Internationally recognized Japanese scientist Masaru Emoto documented his research findings on the vibrational impact of words, thoughts, and feelings in his book, *The Hidden Messages in Water.*

Dr. Emoto used high-speed photography to show how crystalline structures from frozen water could be changed by focused thoughts directed at them. Positive thoughts and words such as *thank-you* and *gratitude* made beautiful snowflakelike crystal formations. But negative thoughts or words usually did not create any crystals. If any did form, those crystals were partial and distorted. It was interesting to note that Elvis Presley's song "Heartbreak Hotel" played to the water produced a crystal that was partially split in two. When the water was exposed to the energy of microwave ovens, television, rap music, and the word *devil*, instead of crystals, dark, bloblike structures formed.

Spirit continues,

> *The Oneness is like an image of the Creator. It is not the Creator but only a piece of Him with a high energy vibration. Actually, the Creator is best represented for being in the middle of the infinity sign where the points touch and the lines cross. As the infinity spiral expands, the outer edges get denser and the energy vibration decreases as it slows down. But what is above is below. However, it is not truly up and down but rather to the right and left*

while going in all directions at once, hence the infinity sign.
The Creator is infinite. [See illustration 1.]

Multiple entities of the Christian God—the Father, the Son, and the Holy Spirit—do not exist as separate beings like you may have been taught. They are all one. The Oneness exists as a group energy within the light world. Consciousness is plural and multifaceted and so is the Oneness. It's like a singular ocean which contains many drops of water, a whole made up of multiple drops. The Oneness is only singular according to humankind's perception. The confusion comes from how the Creator has been presented in certain religions. When religion speaks of the deity, it does not speak of Oneness, so humanity has not learned to think of the Creator in the singular.

It is said that St. Patrick explained Christianity to the pagan king of Ireland by using the three leaf clover as an example. He noted that each of the three leaves represented one aspect of the Trinity—the first leaf was God, the second was the Son of God, and the third leaf was the Holy Spirit—with the stem unifying them all.

I believe that the three leaf clover lends itself well to clarifying the spiritual model of existence shown to me by my guides. It also fits with the Native American version of the interconnection among all lives. As you visualize the three leaf clover, the central leaf stands for God/the Great

Spirit/Creator. The leaf on the left exemplifies all the entities who have souls—the children of God. The remaining leaf on the right is the symbol for all the nature spirits who do not have souls. (For more information see chapter 11, "Dimensions of Consciousness.") Finally, the stem is the unifying element that shows our relationship with the others.

Spirit continues,

> Over time, many messengers have been sent to mankind, such as Jesus, who was a great messenger and healer. The reason he is called the Son is because the messenger is a child of the Creator. He is also called the Sun because he was the bringer of light/enlightenment to humanity. Spirit is the life force that has created all things. But Spirit is also the Oneness as the expression of light. Jesus did not come to Earth to start Christianity; that was not his purpose. Jesus's purpose was to be a healer and a teacher. His purpose and mission was to link people to the Creator so they could remember where they were from. To see Jesus as just a man is to see an image instead of the Spirit within.

> However, when the people killed Jesus, they formed a religion in his honor to help atone for their actions. The purpose of his sacrifice was to show people that there is more than just the physical form. He died so that he could rise again in three days and show that Spirit cannot be destroyed. Upon death, Spirit is released from the physical form when that form ceases to function. Humankind has been shown this lesson over and over. But most humans still do not understand, are in denial, or have no concept of the nature of Spirit and the Spiritual Dimension.

I have repeatedly heard minister state that Jesus said, "I am the resurrection and the way. You cannot enter heaven except through me," My guides tell me that He was saying that the way to God is though Spirit and that people needed to follow His example to reconnect to the light. Not in the physical body sense but in what He represented—the light and the spiritual path of life. This is the same path as what the Native Americans call the Red Road.

The Creator also sent other emissaries such as the Buddha, Krishna, and others, not to start religions but to help people reconnect with Spirit in various places and times. These messages varied based on the lifestyle, needs, and understanding of humanity in a specific time and place. The people then linked to their version of the Creator through the messenger sent to Earth. As a result, there are multiple manners of worship. Consider the ways of the Hindus, Muslims, Buddhists, Jews, etc. Each had an emissary, an enlightened soul from the Oneness whose message and purpose were the same—to bring enlightenment, teachings, healing, and the reconnecting to Spirit. All came from the same place, the Oneness. I have heard these emissaries' Spirit referred to as the Christ Consciousness.

Spirit continues,

> *The original visions were all generated from the Oneness and at one time the information was pure. But the original messages have become distorted. Religious writings have been translated inaccurately. Other "agendas" have been added. Some religious groups have become far removed from their original beliefs.*

Over the years, time has distorted the truth and the original messages as well. All religions are looking for the truth and to find the way to evolve spiritually. But some individuals and religions have lost their focuses and believe war is the only answer to accomplishing their goals. The Roman Catholic Crusades are a good example of the sidetracking, but there are many others.

Often religions are used by individuals and/or groups of individuals to control society and create a structure that benefits them. Anything that does not fit within their framework or threatens their belief system is deemed as evil in origin or nature. The faithful are warned to stay away from "the evil" in fear of eternal damnation. Notice how often the leaders of several religious groups claim to hold all the answers and everyone else is wrong. This is not logical and definitely not how the Creator meant things to be.

A Wake-Up Call!

The meaning of the word *religion* is to realign with God. But there are many ways to realign, just as there are many pathways (religions) to travel when attempting to reconnect to the Creator. However, all the pathways lead to the same destination, the Oneness. So it is immaterial which path you take or belief system you use if you are connecting to the light of the Oneness and living by the Spiritual Law.

CHAPTER 4

The Universal Codes of Life

Humankind has not woven the web of life. We are but one thread in it. Whatever we do to the web, we do to our selves. All things are bound together. All things connect.

—Chief Seattle, 1855

Humanity has two sets of laws to consider when making life choices:

1. Universal spiritual laws known as the Universal Codes of Life.
2. Physical and religious laws of human material existence.

Universal Codes of Life

The Universal Codes of Life exist to bring balance and harmony to the Universe. Humanity needs to understand how these Universal Laws relate to our earthly laws. The Universal Codes are similar to the Christian Ten Commandments; however, the Codes exist on an expanded, holistic level that encompasses all life everywhere, not just humanity. By comparison, the Ten Commandments are equivalent to doing personal life-purpose work while the Codes represent global-purpose work, as previously discussed in chapter 2. However, humanity always has free will to choose whether or not to follow each set of laws.

For example, commandment six in the Bible states that we "shall not kill" (Exodus 20:13). In the Ten Commandments this is interpreted to apply to human life. But mankind makes exceptions for social needs based on human judgment.

The Universal Codes coordinate with the laws of nature, expanding the "no killing" concept to respecting and valuing all life everywhere. Spiritual Law allows killing to meet one's physical survival needs. The cycle of birth and death functions in all of nature. Predators kill and eat other animals as a means of survival—an acceptable law of nature. However, killing for the sake of killing itself is not respecting other life and that breaks the Spiritual Law.

Spirit explains,

> *It is important to understand the full meaning of the Universal Codes of Life and to live within their guidelines. But at the same time, one must also exist in the physically material world. By functioning in both the spiritual and physical worlds, humankind builds a bridge between these two parallel realms. The physical and spiritual worlds are mirror images of each other. However, at all times it is important to maintain a balance between personal-growth work on the physical level and work in the spiritual world.*

Avoid getting caught up in the following behaviors:

1. Some individuals have such a strong spiritual commitment that it can lead to neglect of the physical body and other worldly responsibilities. Enthusiastic people may spend hours in meditation or other spiritual practices while neglecting their homes, their families, their bodies, or their social contacts. Even taking the time to play or relax as a balance is forgotten.

2. On the opposite extreme are those individuals who focus only on activities that result in material gain. These people may work fourteen or more hours each day, trying to acquire more prestige, money, and power. Taking the time for spiritual practices such as prayer, meditation, or spending time in nature would be considered a waste of time. Often families don't see one of their members very often because that person is "too busy making a living." Even if you love your job, take time for other activities to maintain an overall balance.

Neither of the above extremes is good. Keep in mind that to grow in spiritual awareness, you must achieve balance in all areas of life. Psychology tells us that there are four main expressions of life function that we must work on simultaneously:

- mental—learning, planning, organizing, stimulating the intellect
- emotional—social interactions and contacts, love interests, enjoyment, self-respect
- physical—work, play, food, sleep, exercise
- spiritual—prayer, meditation, worship, spiritual exercises

As a therapist, I find that those who are the happiest with their lives are functioning well, or reasonably well, in all of the four areas. Those with three high functioning areas manage quite well most of the time. However, if there are only one or two levels of adequate performance, they get depressed and life is troubled. It's like sitting on a four-legged stool. If you have a one short leg on the stool, you can still balance on the three good ones. If more than one leg is short, your balance becomes very difficult. Test yourself to see what needs work.

Society has developed cultural, physical, and religious laws that help us stay in balance.

The Ten Commandments

The Ten Commandments from the Bible (Exodus 20: 1–17) were given to the Jews through Moses on Mount Sinai (Exodus 19:20). They are listed in the Old Testament, but their message applies to all mankind. The commandments are life lessons. Each one is a separate lesson about a different aspect of life, such as killing, communication, honoring, etc. For those who are connected to Spirit and the light, this overview of the commandments defines the way to live one's life and stay in balance.

According to the Star Council of Light,

> *The commandments listed in the Bible are not explained as completely as necessary. The vibration of the words is not being interpreted correctly today.*

The following list is the Spiritual interpretation of the commandments, based on the Codes of Life as explained by the Council:

Commandment 1: "Thou shalt have no other God's before me."

The Spiritual interpretation:

- Acknowledge God's existence and His connection to everything that is, the Oneness.
- Do not worship the messengers that have come before, such as the Buddha, Jesus, Mohammed, among others.
- Honor nature, both masculine and feminine energies, but do not perceive them as God. There are many paths (religions/belief systems), but they all lead to the Oneness.
- Value your spiritual connection above all other things (e.g., money, power, personal images).

The seven deadly sins designated by Roman Catholic Pope Gregory I can be seen as putting something else before God, so they serve as examples to the violation of this commandment. The deadly sins are lust, gluttony, greed, sloth, wrath, envy, and pride.

Commandment 2: "Thou shalt not make unto thee any graven image or likeness of anything that is in heaven above or in the earth beneath ..."

The Spiritual interpretation:

- Do not worry about what God looks like, based on what you have been taught. God is in the Oneness, the loving energy, the creative force, and the only way to experience God is from within you. The image of God is like looking into a mirror; you only see the reflection of what is within you. Again, if you see the figure of the man, then you are seeing the image, but if you see what is within that figure, then you are seeing God.

- God is unconditional love and acceptance without judgment or punishment. Do not be deceived by the distortions popularized by religions. Do not fear God.

Commandment 3: "Thou shalt not take the name of the Lord thy God in vain ..."

The Spiritual interpretation:

- Speak God's name from the heart and soul only. God's name has the vibration of the Word, as mentioned earlier. When your words are not spoken through your heart, it is like taking the Lord's name in vain by using it in a swearing phrase. Imagine God within yourself and within all things. Have proper respect.

Commandment 4. "Remember the Sabbath day, to keep it holy ..."

The Spiritual interpretation:

- The seventh day is a symbolic time for prayer from your heart. But in reality each day is a Sabbath. Living each day as if it was the Sabbath is important. Do not set only one day aside to honor and worship the Creator.

- Appreciate life and all your blessings. It is important to pray and honor every day, in the morning and in the evening, not just once a week. Pray for "the highest good" for all things and honor everything that is alive. Pray for the Universe, for Mother Earth, and Father Sky like the indigenous cultures, not just for your own personal needs.

- Honor all relationships and the planet. You can pray anywhere and at any time, not just in church. The most important factor is praying from your heart. Do not pray as an impersonal mouthing of specific words, as done in a rote ritual. God hears all sincere prayers. Ceremony and prayers are very important.

Commandment 5: "Honor thy father and mother ..."
The Spiritual interpretation:
- This does not only address one's physical mother and father but also the Mother Earth and Father Sky, the atmosphere and All That Is, all that exists. It also means to not do anything that would damage the planet or other beings.

Indigenous belief systems and origin stories always work in collaboration with Mother Earth and Father Sky. They consider these two to be as important as the human parents, if not more so. Perhaps we should all consider how our actions are impacting the environment we live in. It is an often accepted fact that gardeners who talk to their plants and flowers get better results and a more prolific yield. I think this would be considered a way of honoring the earth. If so, what does that tell you about the need to honor the earth and the sky on a more consistent basis? We are all truly connected.

Commandment 6: "Thou shalt not kill ..."
The Spiritual interpretation:
- Honor life and live within honor. When an individual chooses the darkness over light, he helps to destroy the earth. Do not cause injury; this is a Universal Law, a sacred commitment.

How many species of plants and animals are endangered or extinct as a direct result of human action and pollution? The Bible tells us that in the beginning God gave humans dominion over the land and all upon it with instructions to " ...replenish the earth and subdue it" (Genesis 1:26–28). Have we overdone it or misinterpreted the commandment?

Picking a flower in the field, only to throw it away after sniffing it can be considered killing it because one creates a waste of the beauty as the flower dies on the ground without water or its root connection. In some belief systems, stepping on an ant is not acceptable.

Commandment 7: "Thou shalt not commit adultery ..."
The Spiritual interpretation:
- Honor marriage and recognize the relationship that has been given to you as a gift. That relationship is a connection of spirit and the earth. The male and the female are the two natural forces of Spirit. The female represents matter, and male is spirit energy, and they come together to create the whole and to perpetuate life.
- This is the creative relationship that embraces one's commitment to another individual and the relationship one has with Spirit.

This commandment relates to the need for male and female to recognize that they are parts of the whole and both are equally important. Honor each other, and when the lessons are learned from a particular relationship, feel free to move on to another relationship. Adultery comes from not honoring each other or recognizing the need to learn lessons inherent in the relationship.

Commandment 8: "Thou shalt not steal ..."
The Spiritual interpretation:

- This commandment deals with greed and not taking that which does not belong to you in any way or manner.
- It also implies that it is important to give when you have the opportunity to do so. The Law of the Universe says, "When one gives, one is working in relationship with creation." Giving and receiving are equal parts of the Sacred Circle.

Another way of looking at "stealing" is to consider what we are not doing to help others in need. If we do not volunteer time or money to people or groups who serve others, is that not stealing through selfish, self-serving behavior? Native American legends have many stories about coyote or spider (*Iktome*) and their selfish behaviors. These stories are designed to teach everyone, especially children, the importance of integrity, community, and the need to work together for the benefit of all.

Commandment 9: "Thou shalt not bear false witness …"
The Spiritual interpretation:
- Speak only what is true at all times.
- Since words have power, you must speak only in a positive and collaborative manner.

The power of our words is immense and far reaching. Parents sometimes tell a child that he is worthless, ugly, dumb, bad, especially when they are angry at the child. The recipient of those negative comments learns to believe them. I have had a number of clients who had a great deal of old programming from their childhood to unlearn. These types of messages can easily fit into this commandment, in my opinion.

Commandment 10: "Thou shalt not covet thy neighbor's house ..."

The Spiritual interpretation:

- It is important to be grateful for one's blessings. Feeling and expressing sincere gratitude is the key to receiving.
- You must honor what you have been given instead of desiring another's possessions. You must earn what is given to you, what you receive.

In this case, "earning" refers to living life in such a manner that things like peace of mind, friendships, and love are earned, not just bought with money. Money has substantial limits on what it can purchase, but even money has to be earned in traditional ways.

A Wake-Up Call!

The Codes of Life is an expanded version of the Ten Commandments representing guidelines on how to live to maintain balance and harmony in life.

As each soul becomes more awake and aware, it has an obligation to fulfill one's life purpose on all three levels:

1. Accomplishing one's life purpose on a personal level. The spiritual interpretation is that you learn to make personal sacrifices to help others live.
2. Accomplishing one's purpose on a friends/family and global scale would be to teach about life and what life really is. Life is the manifestation of the experience. First you have a personal experience. Then you share the experience with your family and friends.
3. Finally you take that wisdom to a larger, global scale.

CHAPTER 5

Prayer

The trouble with our praying is, we do it as a last resort.
—Will Rogers

Prayer is another Code of Life, according to the Council:

Learn how to speak to the Creator. Then learn to listen so you can receive the message from the Creator. Prayer is speaking whatever is in your heart directly to God, and in that manner it is heard. Prayer is very strong.

Through the centuries, the ability to connect to Spirit has been misused. Some people have worshiped false idols or used other people to connect their prayers to the Creator. Prayer is meant to be direct, a personal connection. Receiving an answer to prayer is also a direct and personal experience. Do not go through intermediaries, whose purpose is to distance you from the Creator. You may pray in a group where everyone entering the prayer circle is of like heart and mind. You can also pray at any time in your own personal manner. However, it is important to pray from your heart, not just utter rote words. When you pray, focus on the positive.

The Lord's Prayer is exemplary, but you must also have your own personal prayer. Everyone needs his own way of praying in addition to uttering the Lord's Prayer. Say whatever is in your heart. Much of mankind believes that if someone speaks to the Creator, that the Creator will not speak back. Pray, and within that prayer you will find your understanding and answer. Any prayer format can work, but it is important to close each prayer by saying thank you and being grateful for all the blessings in your life.

Prayer is necessary every day of your life. When you pray and ask for help, you are acknowledging the Spirit, the Creator, and the Universe. You are thanking the Creator every time you pray. Through prayer you acknowledge that there is help within this world, that there is a higher power: the Creator. But when you pray, you must open your heart and open your hands. If you ask for help, open your own hands and be ready to receive the requested help.

Prayer is a form of meditation, and the individual consciousness will evolve to the higher vibration as a result. If prayer is not included in daily life, then the evolution of the soul to higher consciousness will not continue. Pray daily. Make it a personal ritual to pray in the morning and in the evening. Thank the sun, moon, and stars for rising and then setting as they bring light to the earth. Do this as you pray for the highest good of the earth, for all people, and your family and friends. Prayer is much stronger than most people realize.

One prayer can send very strong vibrations of energy throughout the Universe. So imagine what would happen if many people prayed together at one time. Life is spoken in a prayer. Ritual and ceremony are important for healing and building the Sacred Circle. When you pray from your heart, the Sacred Circle becomes stronger and helps all humanity.

In his book, *Healing Words*, Larry Dossey talks about the modalities and effects of prayer research done at the Spindrift Institute. The mission of the Spindrift Institute is to promote research in the field of prayer, consciousness, and spiritual healing. For more information, visit their website at www.spindriftresearch.org.

Dossey states that research shows that praying for the "highest good" of a situation had a more positive result than just praying for a certain situation to change. However, both prayer methods appeared to generate positive results.

Praying for the highest good of a situation allows the Universe to make the call on what is best in a situation. For example, someone is very ill, and friends are praying in an effort to help. However, some are praying for the friend to get better quickly while others are praying to let them die and others for a slow recovery so the ill friend can get rested from a busy schedule. These prayers are in direct opposition to each other and consequently not useful to the ill person.

An experience I had many years ago with a simple sincere prayer left me astounded and convinced that prayer works.

I was chatting with a friend at a bar we often frequented. I usually drank a Bacardi cocktail out of companionship but felt no real desire for alcohol. Then one day after ordering my drink I suddenly craved that drink and couldn't wait to have it set down in front of me. This truly surprised and scared me because I realized that craving a drink is a sign of alcoholic addiction. I quickly and sincerely asked the Creator to please help me not want the drink. Instantly, the craving went away and has never returned. I now drink on occasion but have never had a problem with alcohol. I firmly believe that experience was to help me learn a life lesson. I made a choice that day without even realizing it, a choice to follow the light instead of the shadow side.

A Wake-Up Call!

Prayer from the heart is a wonderful way to unload the worldly weight off your shoulders, even if the answer you want doesn't come instantly or in the way you anticipate it. Prayer is an important connection to the Creator, and it is always heard. If it is sincere, it can accomplish miracles.

PART 2

The Beginning

CHAPTER 6

What Is Dark Energy and How Did It Come to Be?

Remember this. When people choose to withdraw from a fire, the fire continues to give warmth, but they grow cold. When people choose to withdraw from the light, the light continues to be bright in itself, but they are in the darkness. This is also the case when people withdraw from God.

—Augustine

Spirit tells me the following story:

Your earth came to exist at the beginning of time when a war took place in heaven and there was a fallen angel [Revelation 20: 7–9] who existed in the same place as the Oneness. The fallen angel became known in legends as the devil, Lucifer, Hades, Apollo, and the Dark Sun.

Literature has many names for this fallen angel and frequently his name has become synonymous with the name for the underworld, Hades.

The darkness grew out of light consciousness that had free will and because of that made the choice for power. At the start, one harmless cell veered off. Then the cell grew, became distorted, and developed into the shadow consciousness. The fallen angel is like a force, a distortion, or a cancerous cell that continues to multiply and grow.

This force has taken on a life of its own and is known today as the shadow or the dark side. The original veering off created a separation from Spirit and the eventual manifestation of the shadow. Lucifer then convinced other souls that they too did not need God and could make their own decisions. This was the beginning of the war between the light and the darkness.

Some understand the significance of that war through what is taking place on Earth. While others think perhaps it is not really happening or it is not important. Your earth was created for choice making, and now is the time to choose which side to affiliate with—the light or the dark. However, if you are not connected to the light, in the absence of light, darkness prevails in your life. If you are connected to the light, then you are called a light worker.

The Light, the Oneness, is also known as Creator, God, Jehovah, Allah, the Great Spirit, etc. But in reality, it's all one and the same. Humans simply call the One by different names based on their particular belief systems.

For a long time there was a membrane separating the forces of light and darkness. But now that membrane is gone, and the forces are colliding. What kept them separate in the past was the fact that indigenous cultures had a strong connection to the light through their ceremonies. Over time these cultures and their spiritual practices have been almost forgotten or destroyed. So consequently, the protective Sacred Circle created to connect and hold humankind in the light has also dissipated.

The Sacred Circle can no longer hold the light on Earth. The balance between the light and dark forces no longer exits. All of the earth's natural forces are out of control, which results in massive lack of light consciousness and destruction. [See chapter 16, "Cleansing Storms."]

Regularly at night, I dreamed about the violence, death, and destruction happening on Earth. In these dreams, I am usually an observer, but I am also a participant. The dual role is the result of my connecting into the energy of Mother Earth along with my relating to the energy of the pain and suffering of others. The vibration of what is happening on Earth goes into the energy field of the earth, and many who are sensitive can recognize and access it. In psychology, this is known as the *stream of consciousness*. My dreams about war, killing, bombs, etc., always leave me upset because they seem so real and emotionally charged. I've asked for help to deal with them, and Spirit has responded by putting a shield around me so I no longer experience them as often or with so much intensity.

Positive things are happening as well. These include the re-emergence of the awareness of the Star Nation, the revival of sacred ceremonies, and the return of the ancient spiritual practices on several Native American reservations. The Sioux Sun Dances are drawing participants and observers from all over the world. Sweat lodge practices are becoming more and more common. There can be a reuniting of the Sacred Hoop. This reuniting will then return balance and harmony to Earth and humankind.

A Wake-Up Call!

The earth was created to give souls a choice to affiliate with the light or the dark energy. The time for choosing is now. Earth's population is expanding exponentially as souls are coming here to make that choice.

CHAPTER 7

What Is the Star Nation?

We do not inherit the earth from our ancestors. We borrow it from our children.

—Native American proverb

The Light Council states,

> *All of the worlds that exist in the universal creation are part of the Star Nation, and all are connected to the Oneness. As the information is revealed and shared with others, humankind will understand that they are from the stars and are part of the Star Nation. Earth is just one of the many different worlds in the Universe that have life on them. These worlds are at different points in their spiritual evolutions.*
>
> *In Atlantis, everyone still had the star communication ability. In the past we have spoken to the Atlanteans, the*

Egyptians, the Native American medicine people, and many others. Native American men and women and other wisdom keepers are now being told by their spirit guides that the time has come for them to share their hidden information with the rest of humankind.

As a comparison, the Star Nation is like the Federation of Planets from the Star Trek television series, only much larger in scope. The light of consciousness that humankind needs for spiritual growth on Earth comes from the stars, as discussed in this book's introduction.

The Star Connection

According to the Council,

- *In ancient Egypt, there still were quite a few star priests and priestesses who could communicate with the stars. They could also do dimensional travel and bring the star energy information back to Earth.*

Indigenous legends also provide several examples:

- The Lakota, Navajo, Hopi, and other tribes had medicine men known as Star Shamans. These Star Shamans communicated with beings from the stars and brought that information to Earth.
- The Hopi have a Star Katchina and a Star Ceremony.
- Mayans speak about the Sky People and believe they are from the Pleiades star system.
- The Navajo have a star chant as part of their religion. They believe it was given to them by the star beings.

- Many of the Native American tribes such as Cherokee, Hopi, Osage, Sioux, and others believe they came from the Pleiades constellation.
- The Pawnee also have a Star Ceremony and a star chant given to them by the Star People to bring down the star energy.
- Iroquois believe they once lived in the heavens.
- The Osage origin story talks about living among the stars.
- The Cherokee went to Stone Mountain to perform ceremonies that would connect them to the energy of the Sky Gods.
- Islamic tradition says the stars are called the "breath of the Merciful One (Allah)."

Astronomers have stated that there are 100 billion galaxies in the Universe, and our solar system is located in the Milky Way Galaxy. Presently, Earth is at a lower level of consciousness. However, before 2012—the Mayan date of change—many people will need to develop a higher consciousness level so that the coming shift of consciousness can be more positive.

The Sacred Hoop spoken about by the Native Americans will be rejoined and then the leaves will begin to return to the Sacred Tree of Life spoken about by Black Elk in *Black Elk Speaks*. The Sacred Circle is the way the star energy of light consciousness is currently brought to Earth. More information on this is available in chapter 9, "The Tree of Life."

A Wake-Up Call!

The Light Council says,

> *In all of the Universe, there is a Oneness that connects all life everywhere, not just on this world. There are many other worlds that have life on them, in addition to the earth.*

CHAPTER 8

What Is the Connection Between the Stars and Humankind?

Angels are spiritual energy.

—Alexis F. Hope

According to the Light Council,

> *In the Universe, there is and always has been nonphysical matter light energy, which is consciousness. Consciousness then creates more consciousness like a cell dividing. As life continues to grow, the cell cluster becomes greater in size. The physical world was formed as consciousness becomes aware of itself.*

In her book *Other Campfires Were Here Before Ours*, Cherokee author Jamie Sams describes consciousness becoming aware of itself and how the world was formed.

The Council continues,

> *Humans are a highly developed consciousness which is not indigenous to Earth. Some of those who originally came to Earth were of higher consciousness, others were not. Eons ago, beings from many dimensions came to Earth. Some of these beings were from a whole different solar system. Others came from a black hole that acts as portal to a different solar system.*

Within the pages of *You Are Becoming a Galactic Human*, authors Virginia Essence and Sheldon Nidle contend that the Syrians were involved in bringing the earth humans here from the Vega Star System. According to this text, the Syrian influence began two million years before Christ in Hyburnia and Lemuria. That influence ended when Atlantis destroyed Lemuria out of jealousy about the Lemurian trade routes and the importance of those routes within the world the Lemurians had settled.

The Council adds,

> *The very first beings on Earth were nonhumans of much lower energy vibration and more physical density. The humans with souls were put on Earth later to be the keepers of the earth. They are called Indians, also known as the Native Americans.*

Edgar Cayce, the famous twentieth century American clairvoyant, also talked about red man first appearing on Earth in Atlantis and North America.

In *The Voices of Our Ancestors*, Cherokee author Dhyani Ywahoo states that according to oral tradition, the Cherokee consider themselves to be the original earth people. They believe angelic beings created the earth and its people as a place of choice and learning. According to the Cherokee, the descendants of the Pleiadeans and the earth beings are called the Red Nations of North America. Their history tells of the Pleiadean Star People coming to Atlantis, intermingling with the original earth inhabitants, and having children that carried the beginnings of higher consciousness.

The Council confirms that star beings came to Atlantis from the Pleiades:

> *Their purpose was to help bring light into the world and raise human vibratory rate to a higher frequency. Within the center of the Pleiades, there is a doorway into the Oneness, the spiritual dimension, and the star world.*

In many ways, literary accounts and the Council's information also fit with what we have been told about Greek and Roman mythology. It would seem that beings from the Pleiades were sent to Earth to help develop the light consciousness of humankind. These beings had great abilities unknown on Earth and consequently through legends became known as the Greek and Roman gods. The Bible states in Genesis 6:4, "There were giants in the earth in those days. Also after that, when the sons of God came into the daughters of men, and they bore children to them ..."

From religious to historical and New Age literature, there is an abundance of references to the seven stars of the Pleiades. The Pleiades are located in the Milky Way, five hundred light years from the earth. Cross-cultural origin myths also seem to support the theory that beings from the Pleiades could have come to Earth and influenced the development of humankind. For example,

- the Koran relates that the angel Gabriel came from the Pleiades to teach Mohammed and give him laws to live by;
- the Navajo origin story talks about the emerging people finding a Dark God on Earth who claimed to be from the seven stars;
- the Sioux story of the White Buffalo Calf Woman notes that she had a pipe in her left hand and a stone with the seven stars on it in her right hand. Their oral tradition states that the stars were called the holy breath of the Great Spirit, *Wakan Tanka*.

There are numerous Biblical references to the seven stars, as well, and all are found in the book of Revelation:

- "The one who holds the seven stars in his right hand." (Revelation 1:16)
- "The mystery of the seven stars which thou sawest in my right hand and the seven golden candle sticks. The seven stars are the angels of the seven churches …" (Revelation 1:20)
- "These things saith he that hath the seven Spirits of God and the seven stars: I know thy works, that thou hast a name that thou livest …" (Revelation 3:1)

Each of the seven stars represents one of the Sioux Sacred Ceremonies to be performed. To learn more about the ceremonies taught by the White Buffalo Calf Woman, read *Mother Earth Spirituality* by Ed "Eagle Man" McGaa or *The Sacred Pipe,* Black Elk's account of the Seven Rites of the Oglala Sioux, recorded and edited by Joseph Epes Brown.

As the indigenous tribes observed the movement of the sun through the constellations, they were receiving spiritual instructions. Oral tradition then interpreted the observations while the earth and star maps told them what ceremonies to perform in which specific locations.

Early indigenous people believed the ceremonies they performed on Earth were also being performed simultaneously in the spirit world. From this belief came the indigenous concept of *as above, so below.* The ceremonies were thought to connect the spirits in the sky to the humans on Earth. This made the ceremonies like a prayer, so sacred power could then be drawn down from the stars and humankind would be attuned to the will of Wakan Tanka (God).

A Wake-Up Call!

Look at the night sky, search for the Pleiades, and consider how much more those seven stars meant to the early residents of Earth. Humanity's connection is still there among the stars and so is our original home.

CHAPTER 9

The Tree of Life—
Chakra Spirit Connection

*As the poet said, "Only God can make a tree"—probably
because it's so hard to figure out how to get the bark on.*
—Woody Allen

You may be wondering how information can be transmitted from the
star beings and the Universe to mankind. One method is through
the body's chakra system, using crystals that exist within the physical
human body.

The Council states,

> *Crystals bring light energy from the stars directly into the
> earth. They are infused with light so people can connect to
> them directly and consequently experience their own star
> connection. Crystals contain color vibration frequencies*

that work like star wave bands or radio frequency bands.
[Crystal radios also operate through quartz crystal
vibrations.]

Humankind carries many tiny crystals within their bodies.
These crystals can facilitate a connection using the minerals
and magnetic energy intrinsic within the human body.

The Chakra System

The human body has multiple subtle energy centers throughout.
Seven of these centers are considered the body's chakra system. This
system is also called an individual's Tree of Life by the Hindus because
it creates a spiritual link to the Universe and all that exists. The chakras
are connected to the endocrine gland system and are invisible circular
wheels of energy that spin clockwise when they are open, in the same
way that a car's wheels spin on the road.

The chakra centers create the body's own Sacred Energy Circle by
bringing light energy of the rainbow's spectrum from the stars to the
earth and taking the earth's energy back to the Universe. The chakras
are linkage points that bring the vibration of the universal star message
into the physical being. They serve as electrical step-down transformers
to convert the high vibration star energy to the lower level of the human
body. They open and close depending on a person's environmental and
emotional circumstances. This Sacred Energy Circle makes it possible
for us to join into the interconnection of All That Is and receive messages
from the spirit dimension. (See illustration 2 of the yoga poses showing
chakras.)

Contrary to popular belief, the universal energy's chakra entry point into the human body starts at the head, not the feet as often illustrated. The energy then continues to flow down from the head, through the remaining chakra centers, down into the feet where it connects one to the earth. The following path is the light energy progression through the chakra system:

- The *crown chakra* center is on top of the head at the same spot as a newborn's soft spot.
- *Third eye chakra* center is located above the brow in the middle of the forehead.
- *Throat chakra* center is at the lower part of the throat.
- *Heart chakra* center is located midsternum at the level of the heart.
- *Solar plexus chakra* is in the center of the body, a little above the navel for women and at the navel for men.

- *Sacral chakra* center is located at the sacrum, your pelvic area.
- *Base chakra* center, also called the *Root chakra* center, is located at the base of the spine.

After the star energy has completed its path down through the body and into the earth, the Sacred Circle is completed as the energy of the earth rises from the feet and comes back up through the chakra energy centers. Now the energy starts with the feet and the base/root chakra. This returning energy is also known as the kundalini energy. It moves upward through the sacral, the solar plexus, the heart, throat, and third eye and out the crown chakra, reconnecting you back to the Universe.

A person's chakras carry the full spectrum of the rainbow, starting with red at the base chakra, orange in the sacral area, yellow at the solar plexus, green for the heart, light blue for the throat, indigo blue for the third eye, and finally purple at the crown. Above the crown is a white universal light. These colors work together to create a person's biomagnetic energy field, more commonly known as the aura or energy body.

As previously mentioned, universal energy flows down from the crown through your body to the base chakra and into the feet, grounding you to the earth. An individual personifies the Tree of Life, a conduit through which energy, information, and knowledge of healing can flow. This energy exchange is the Sacred Circle, energy coming from the stars, through a person, into the earth, and then back again to the stars in a continuous circular energy pattern.

Chakra Crystals

Following is a list of crystals whose use Spirit has advised to enhance the function of certain chakra energy centers. These stones can be placed directly on the chakra centers to assist a practitioner when doing healing and energy balancing work.

Crown Chakra—Amethyst

The crown chakra, located at the top of the head, is where the universal spiritual energy first enters the body. If the crown chakra is closed or blocked, you are not able to receive spiritual wisdom, guidance, or understanding. If the center is open, you can more easily find your life purpose and pathway. Amethyst resonates with the crown chakra to keep it open, balanced, attuned, and connected to the spiritual realm.

Amethyst represents spirit and contentment. This stone is also very useful in aiding meditation since it transforms lower energies into higher ones.

Third Eye Chakra—Herkimer Diamond

The third eye chakra, located above the brow in the center of the forehead, represents insight. When it is open, it activates the intuitive senses of clairvoyance (clear sight), clairaudience (clear hearing), and clairsencience (clear sensing) as it interprets the spiritual information. The third eye chakra functions to read the universal energy and then translate it into thoughts.

The Herkimer diamond opens and activates the third eye. It stimulates the intuitive senses and enhances spiritual guidance and development through conscious thought. Herkimer is useful to wear as a pendant because it helps to generate a protective field around the wearer. However, it should not be worn for twenty-four-hour periods at a time. Take it off when you sleep because it can be disruptive when worn incessantly. Herkimer diamond is also known as the stone of attunement to Spirit or to another human being. In addition, it is helpful in dispelling toxins from the body.

Throat Chakra—Lapis Lazuli

The throat chakra is a spiritual communications center. When it is open, you can communicate wisdom and understanding to others. This chakra broadcasts spiritual energy in the form of sound, so it can help others open their own chakras. Speak the truth because truth is light, and light is the spiritual energy. As spiritual energy comes in through the crown chakra, it is transmitted through the throat chakra to express light in the world.

Lapis is the blue stone whose vibration facilitates the opening of the throat chakra. It has been said to help one gain insight into the unknown mysteries to provide enhanced wisdom.

Heart—Rose Quartz

The heart chakra represents unconditional love. As spiritual energy enters, it stimulates you to receive and express love to others. If the chakra is closed or blocked, then you will wither because the human heart needs love to nourish the soul.

Rose quartz, as the name implies, is pink, and it represents the universal realm. This crystal helps individuals to open up and connect to the energy of love with relationships, families, and friendships.

Solar Plexus—Green Fluorite

The solar plexus chakra is where spiritual energy meets earth energy, and the chakra integrates the two energetic polarities to create balance in the personality. This is the chakra of feelings and emotions. If there is a blockage in the solar plexus, it can cause the personality to experience negative emotions and confusion. Fear, guilt, shame, and a sense of abandonment are some of the emotions that could result from a blockage. Some people may even experience a personality split accompanied by a sense of loss of purpose and of life's meaning. Without the integration of the spiritual and physical energies, there exists a sense of being disconnected from oneself and the Universe.

Green fluorite opens the solar plexus chakra, which allows the infusion of Spirit into the conscious mind and helps with balancing, healing, and spiritual integration. The color green carries a healing energy vibration. Fluorite absorbs and cleanses emotional upset and confusion from your energy field.

Sacral Chakra—Black Tourmaline

The sacral chakra integrates universal energy and is the creative center of the body. Physically, it concentrates spiritual essence into the egg and the sperm to create new life. Psychologically, it organizes thoughts into patterns that bring creativity into one's consciousness. It also creates the magnetic force of attraction between male and female. Creative energy becomes inspiration and gives birth to consciousness expressed in words and actions.

Consciousness allows mankind to live in harmony with nature through honoring, expressing, and living life with respect and love for the Creator and His creation. This creative force lies within all humankind. When you recognize it, you enter into the Circle of Life. Every thought, word, and deed impacts the whole. If you move one grain of sand, you have altered the Universe. The power of creation is in your hands, and you can use it wisely or foolishly.

If the sacral chakra is blocked, your creativity and action is disorganized and lacks conscious awareness. Without inspiration, life becomes a routine instead of an adventure because the Circle of Life is broken.

Black tourmaline helps bring creative energy back into manifestation. It protects by helping your thought processes focus and block external interference that can distract you from your path. It can also absorb negative energy and others' thought forms. Black tourmaline helps bring energy through your body and release it at this chakra. It is useful to move energy through the body, to cleanse, and release it through your feet.

Root Chakra—Smoky Quartz

The root chakra, located at the base of the spine, creates a connection to the earth like the roots of a tree. It plants an individual so he or she can grow, develop, and learn the lessons of life. Stability and security are the main energies you receive from the earth. A person's place in the world and one's sense of identity are the result of a strong connection to earth energy. The root chakra creates the grounding that brings light into the world. Smoky quartz facilitates the process of grounding you to the earth.

Chakras as the Tree of Life

From a human perspective, within the past century individuals are developing more physical illnesses, emotional problems, and mental difficulties requiring intensive treatment. These developments are caused by blockages in our chakra energy systems. Oriental medicine uses acupressure and acupuncture to clear *chi*, or energy blockages from our body.

In the Introduction, there was a mention of the Sacred Hoop of Life which is also understood as the Tree of Life. Black Elk wrote about a vision he received in his book *Black Elk Speaks* Black Elk stated that the Tree of Life in his vision was crying, disappointed with the actions of humanity. The chakra blockages, with their associated physical problems, can be interpreted as the Tree crying. Humanity is no longer living in balance and harmony with everything that exists.

There is too much greed, anger, violence, and a lack of compassionate, unconditional caring help given to others. The earth is being exploited and the Universal Laws are being ignored.

According to the Council,

> *Ceremony and prayer are needed to bring healthy life back to the Tree. The Sacred Hoop which has been broken by the ongoing conflicts on Earth must be rejoined. But for the Sacred Hoop to remain whole, the Voice of Spirit must be spoken in the world. If it is not spoken and people do not have the opportunity to make the choice between the light or shadow, then the Sacred Hoop will not remain whole.*

As I was writing about the Sacred Tree, I had the following dream. I was in a large public garden. Many people were wandering around, enjoying the sunshine with a sense of joy and love in the air. As I walked down a lush, sweet-smelling garden path, I saw a very large tree that had its branches loaded down with an assortment of spring flowers. Each branch bore a different type of flower in great profusion. Some branches were heavy with apple blossoms, others had an array of cherry blossoms, and still others bore daffodils. There were dozens of types of flowers, some I had never seen before. The fragrance was heady.

The tree in my dream was a symbol of the regeneration possible if we pray daily, raise our consciousness levels, honor All That Is, and consequently bring more light to the earth.

A Wake-Up Call!

Realize that you too are carrying the rainbow within your own body, and seize its power. Pray and visualize the light energy entering your body, grounding into the earth, and bringing the earth energy back up to the stars. If you have chosen the light to affiliate with, know that you are a part of the Sacred Hoop of Life. Stay in the light, visualize it surrounding you, and enjoy the journey of life.

CHAPTER 10

Lemuria and Atlantis

None of us can boast about the morality of our ancestors. The records do not show that Adam and Eve were married.

—Ed Howe

Colonel James Churchward, in *The Lost Continent of Mu*, attributes Lemuria for being the original paradise from which the Biblical Adam and Eve were cast out.

The Council clarifies,

This Paradise was a beautiful garden setting, but over time people only remember fragments of what really happened. Like a memory of something from childhood, the knowledge gets distorted. In reality, Adam represents Spirit, and Eve represents matter. They are symbolic, not physical. Adam and Eve represent the birth of the soul. They also represent the human need for companionship. Adam and Eve are

*symbols of the change of dimensional law—how light can
become matter as its vibration slows down.*

Physics tells us that all matter is an expression of energy. Einstein's famous equation—energy equals matter times the speed of light squared ($E=MC^2$)—shows the relationship between the vibration of energy and physical matter. Matter is composed of atoms that have vibrating protons and electrons orbiting around the nucleus. As their vibration speeds up, solids become liquids and then turn into gas as the vibration of the electrons and protons keeps speeding up. The reverse of this process is also true. As the vibration of the electrons and protons slows down, gas becomes liquid and then goes back to a solid state.

This is what the Star Council of Light was talking about when they said Adam and Eve represent matter and the change of dimensional law. Light energy/consciousness carries the extremely high vibration of the stars, like the gas. When the vibration of light energy slows down, it changes dimensions to become the solid matter of the human body. As the vibration of light energy continues to slow down, it forms rocks, trees, and other matter discussed further in the next chapter.

The Council continues,

> *Lemuria broke into pieces after Atlantis attacked it with
> energy beams generated by crystals. This was not the same
> crystal energy humans know about today. The Atlantian
> energy was similar to an electromagnetic light beam, like
> a laser from the stars. Atlantians were able to move things
> with the electromagnetic energy—an energy so powerful
> that it could run an entire city. This is how large multiton
> stones were moved to build structures.*

Like Lemuria, Atlantis is also under water now because it too broke apart. Humanity had forgotten about this lost world and was reminded when the ancient Greek philosopher Plato wrote about an island called Atlantis. The Atlantians' religion involved the cycles of the seasons. Atlantians had a direct link to the stars through personal telepathic communication.

According to Spirit,

> Atlantians used crystals to tune into the universal energy channel. Their communications network was very advanced. Their telepathic communication and structures stored energy in the earth in a way that set up a perfect balance. The balancing of the energy between the earth and the stars set up an electromagnetic field. This field also produced the atmosphere which allowed human beings to communicate with the stars. Atlantian inner senses were developed, and with all of the twelve DNA strands in place, the Atlantians themselves were good energy conductors.

> Human bodies are made up of water and crystals that match the crystalline structure of earth energy. The Atlantian temple was pyramid shaped, and this design carried over into Egypt. The pyramid shape is an energetic form.

> One reason Atlantis is not fully documented is because those who inhabited Atlantis were originally from the stars. Some Atlantians were warlike and brought with them a tremendous power source that eventually destroyed their nation. These beings conducted genetic engineering

and were able to successfully disconnect all but two of the human DNA strands.

When Atlantis was destroyed, those warlike beings survived. There was a misuse of power and knowledge in Atlantis. However, the information of that time is not forever lost; it was hidden and will be discovered when the time is appropriate.

Because of the human DNA disconnection by the warlike reptilians in Atlantis, humanity needs to raise its consciousness level, connect to Spirit, and reconnect its DNA. This is all part of the waking-up process discussed earlier. That shadow energy is still very active, but do not concern yourself with it because your fear is what gives them more power. Focus instead on visualizing the earth as renewed and humans living in peace, balance, and harmony. Send thoughts of gratitude and love to the oceans, and visualize that energy going down to the bottom of the ocean to cleanse and energize it.

A Wake-Up Call!

There is so much more to the realm of human history than even science fiction writers can imagine. Slowly, pieces of truth are resurfacing. Continue to do your own personal light work as discussed in chapter 2 (your personal purpose) and look forward to some exciting discoveries.

PART 3

Dimensions of Existence

CHAPTER 11

Levels of Consciousness

Angels have no philosophy but love.

—Adeline Collen Ray

There are two distinct types of vibrations in the levels of consciousness:

1. The spiritual realm of light and higher consciousness.
2. The denser dimension of the lower realm.

It is important to recognize that the denser vibration of the lower realm is not the same as the shadow side. The lower realm simply has a different purpose in the overall function of the Universe.

Spirit says,

> *It is not possible to reach the higher levels of consciousness without a soul. The lower dimensional realm is a dense dimension that cannot evolve because there is no light, which is the soul. The lower dimensions have a director/manager composed of low energy who is in charge.*

There are thirteen dimensions, or levels, in the Universe, and everything exists within those dimensions. However, the dimensional borders are not hard and fast dividing lines. There is some level of flexibility and cross over in those boundaries. When you are experiencing the higher vibration levels, you can connect to the higher consciousness and the Oneness even while still in the physical body. However, to make the connection, you must still pray and do personal spiritual growth work. It is not enough to perform service and healing work for others on levels two and three. By being of service to those in need, you are practicing the Universal Law of giving and receiving.

Nonphysical Light Energy

The following list is a general overview of how these dimensions function, based on what I have been shown by my guides.

Nonphysical Level Dimensions

Level thirteen is the highest level possible, with nothing above it. The Universal Council of Light, the Star Council, the Oneness, and the Voice all operate from this level.

Level twelve holds archangel beings and spirit guides who have never had physical bodies.

Level eleven includes spirit guides; however, these guides have had physical bodies at some point in time and are the ascended masters, highly evolved teachers, and angels.

Level ten is the place where humans go when they leave their physical bodies after death if they have made a choice for the light. This is the level where mediums contact those who have "crossed over." Level ten includes spirits who are deceased and healing their own recent past-life traumas.

After completing their own healing, level ten spirits work with living individuals by serving as spirit guides to those on the ninth level.

Physical Level Dimensions

Level nine consists of teachers and healers—humans who have made a choice for the light but are still in a physical body. These individuals are able to use their consciousness to access the tenth level for information, guidance, and healing energy. They use the universal energy that comes through the chakras to open those energy centers and connect to Spirit. Prayer and meditation are very important to individuals whose vibration is on this level.

Level eight is the level for humans still undecided on whether or not to choose the light or the dark side. However, they are praying for higher consciousness. They pray without expecting an answer. These individuals are doing some spiritual work but are praying sparingly, with most of their prayers being for personal survival needs. Individuals at level eight do not have a whole lot of concern for the world as a whole or for the damage done to others. Participants at this level are usually practicing some form of organized religion.

Those people at level seven are even less concerned about prayer and are even more involved with personal survival needs on the planet. They are more concerned with mundane things like making money and accumulating personal possessions. There is no concern with the planet itself or for seeking the higher consciousness. This is an energetically selfish place.

Lower Consciousness

Levels six and below include the lower consciousness dimensions and primitive abilities, as opposed to the higher consciousness levels.

The lower levels are not really physically lower. A better term for them would be a denser elemental and energetic level.

Levels six and lower are inhabited by nonhumans—cats, dogs, farm animals, and wildlife fit into this category. However, the entities at level six still have the opportunity to evolve to higher consciousness and may be part of a group soul consciousness.

Level five is a flatline of existence. Inhabitants of level five are nonhumans that cannot evolve to a higher consciousness level. They can breed to a higher level by affiliating with a higher level human. Once there was a whole civilization living below the earth. It was called the inner earth. Those beings resembled the drawn pictures of the Cro-Magnon man.

Levels four, three, two, and one have made a conscious choice to connect into the lower dimension. These are the dimensions of the earth spirits, the life energy of the location. Crystals, trees, plants, rocks, and water are other examples of the living energies of this dimension.

Earth Spirits

Many books have been written about earth spirits. *Mountains, Meadows and Moonbeams* by Mary Summer Rain is one of these books, but there are many others. Some of these books are in the style of a fairy tale, such as the *Lord of the Ring* series by J. R. Tolkien.

Earth spirits are visible to certain people since the spirits are able to enter the dimension in which humans live. Ancient pagan religions talk about trolls, leprechauns, and an assortment of different kinds of creatures that we now consider mythical. In actuality, these creatures may exist in another energetic dimension.

The Council elaborates on these levels:

In each of these lower four dimensions, there are the special spirits specific to that place. The positive earth spirits are a part of the lower dimensions and serve as the earth protectors. These are creatures such as fairies, sprites, gnomes, etc., who were placed there to watch over and take care of a particular location. Since everything is alive, the spirits are simply the life energy that exists in all things.

The earth spirits/energies are the spirits of the rocks, trees, mountains, water, plus elves and flower spirits, among others. Everything has its own spirit and is alive. The trees, rocks, and water, etc., are not only connected to higher consciousness but also to the earth. The earth spirits have the ability to magnify the energy consciousness that is around them. In a way, they are connected to both heaven and Earth.

Trees, rocks, flowers, and crystals all possess the equivalent of a heart and can be killed. As we have said before, everything on Earth is alive and has its own energy vibration. However, in this dimension the vibration is much lower than that of humanity. The soul of the rock is really the soul of the mountain. Rocks are part of the rock nation. Different territories and regions have different energy sources based on their specific chemical compositions. They all have consciousness, but their various purposes are different from that of humans. Everything is connected to the Sacred Circle. The earth elements that are part of the human body help to create a magnetic balance of all the elements. Everything in creation is interconnected.

Native Americans and other indigenous peoples recognized this concept as an essential part of nature and their belief system.

When a certain consciousness/awareness level is reached, humans are able to communicate with the earth spirits and animals. In order for consciousness to communicate, one needs to be of sincere mind and be able to listen with the mind and heart as well as the ears. Communication is just energy vibration, and it would be beneficial if people learned to listen to the messages. The trees, the animals, and the rocks all have one voice, yet they don't always want to talk. The ocean, lakes, and rivers also have one voice, but they speak in different languages, much like the different languages of mankind.

The human and plant levels of consciousness differ. They represent two dimensions coexisting next to each other, yet they do not overlap or intersect each other. A human communication relationship with animals or elements requires two things: the development of a higher consciousness and the ability to listen. These two things forge the bridge that connects all of the life. In the Oneness, all of life has been one from the beginning. However, as you explore the various dimensions, you can see how they differ from each other.

A Wake-Up Call!

There are extraordinary things that exist, but we cannot see them until we open our minds to the possibilities. For example, little children have not learned to judge and are still open, so their "invisible friends" are only invisible to adults. Consider the possibilities.

CHAPTER 12

Earth-Bound Spirits, Lost Souls, and the Astral Plane

Man was created a little lower than the angels, and has been getting lower ever since.

—Josh Billings

Spirit explains,

> *The astral plane is a place that exists between the dimensions. It's a negative energy "holding place" for many different type of spirits and entities who need help. Being in the astral plane is somewhat like being in limbo or a state of oblivion.*

The following are the types of spirits that can be found in the astral plane, as described by my spirit guides.

Earth-Bound Spirits

After death of the physical form, many souls have become trapped in the astral plane because of their perception of reality and belief of what existence would be like after death. Others remain because of the way in which they died—generally suddenly and/or violently. These spirits are often still attached to the place of their death, perhaps because of strong emotions or other earthly related reasons. Depending on the spiritual growth level of each individual, some may choose to stay in the general location of where they died. That is why hospitals and cemeteries often are connected to stories of spirits or apparitions. These stories represent the "ghosts" known to haunt specific locations.

Freeing such ghosts to continue on their journeys to higher spiritual planes is considered doing personal level two work. Helping another person find the light is also helping that person make the choice between the light and shadow realms so they can bring healing to his or her soul.

Mary Summer Rain writes in detail about her experiences with this type of earth-bound spirits in her book *Phantoms Afoot*. I first learned about this information-packed book in an unusual way. I was standing in a long grocery line, waiting to pay for my purchases, when I started to chat with the woman behind me. I invited her to a Spirit Circle gathering at my house. That evening, she came to the meeting and told me, "This book almost jumped off the shelf at me while I was browsing in a bookstore. I felt very strongly that I was supposed to bring it to you." She then handed me a copy of *Phantoms Afoot*.

This experience is typical of the way that my spirit guides use others to provide me with supplemental information. On several occasions I have had books fall off a library or bookstore shelf and land in front of me. Whatever that book was about was always exactly what

I needed to know. So Spirit works in various and creative ways to give us information.

Lost Souls

The astral plane is also where "lost souls" go after death. They are lost souls because they failed to make the choice to commit to the light or the darkness before their soul left the physical body. Some may have died in a sudden or violent manner such as in a car crash or murder. Others may have been intoxicated or heavily drugged prior to their death. As a result, they did not have the opportunity to choose which side they wanted to be a part of. Often these entities become mischievous spirits. Mischievous spirits are the ones who create noises or move objects in ways that frightens or disturbs humans. These mischievous spirits are also called poltergeists.

They Don't Know They're Dead

Some spirits in the astral plane do not realize that they are dead and no longer have a physical presence. I realized this while attending a shamanic psychopomp workshop after the September 11, 2001, Twin Tower attacks. The teaching focus of the workshop was to help the spirits of the victims cross over to the other side.

The members of our small group participated in a shamanic soul journey, a way of letting our own spirits enter another dimension. Our spirits assembled in what used to be the basement of one of the collapsed towers, where many people were buried as the building came down. We saw spirits everywhere. Some were wandering around; others were hunched over against the walls or lingering in corners. They looked just as they had when still alive. The police and firemen were still dressed in their emergency gear. The office workers wore business suits or dresses, but their energy "felt" different than that of the living. I cannot describe the feeling with words, but intuitively I knew who was dead but whose spirit had not moved on.

I approached a fireman who was sitting on a fallen chunk of concrete by a wall. His head was down so low that I could barely see his face under the helmet. The sadness I felt emitting from him was almost palpable. He did not know he was dead or that he should move on to the light. I asked one of my spirit guides to show him the way, and after a little coaching, I saw him move slowly into the light. My spirit guides and I helped several other victims move on that day, as did the other members of our workshop group. The majority of these deceased souls seemed to be the police officers and firemen who had come to help, only to become victims themselves.

The Bad Ones

For a short time the astral plane also holds those who have committed major crimes against humanity, such as Jim Jones, Hitler, Stalin, Ted Bundy, Saddam Hussein, among others. As we examine history, we can find numerous examples of individuals who fit into the "major crimes against others" category. After a short stay in the astral plane, these spirits wander into the shadow realm of perpetual darkness, based on the information I have been given by my guides.

Caution Is Advised

As a general rule, entities in the astral plane are frequently attracted to living individuals who project light from their aura/electromagnetic energy field. Those who radiate light from their aura are the light workers because they have chosen to connect to the light energy. Often astral plane residents will attach to living individuals using devices such as automatic writing or an Ouji board while the living person tries to contact a spirit guide or seek information from the "other side." It is never advisable to use a spirit guide from the astral plane. These spirits do not have a connection to the Oneness, and they may intentionally mislead any living soul with whom they make contact.

The White Light Shield

When you are trying to make any type of connection to Spirit, it is important to do it in a manner that protects you from making an astral realm connection. Always petition the universal light of the Oneness to seal the area or the room where you are working against all negative energies before starting any spirit connection search. Place a white light shield over the work area while mentally holding the intention of what you are doing and verbally stating out loud with authority something like the following:

"This connection is to the energies that are of the highest vibration and who work for the highest good of All That Is. No others are allowed to enter."

Remember, those of us who are alive have power over the astral spirits, and they can't invade our space if we do not allow them to do so.

Use a white light shield as a protective tool to keep you safe from negative energies. It is a good idea to put such a shield around your home, your car, and yourself, especially when doing meditation or any type of metaphysical work. This is a simple process, and once you have done it several times, it can be accomplished in just seconds. Some people claim it has even protected them from having an accident while driving. There are many variations of this exercise, but here is how it can be accomplished.

Exercise

1. Stand erect with your feet planted about shoulder width apart. Place one hand on your chest and the other on your abdomen. Take several deep breaths, releasing tension, fear, and doubt. Slowly breathe in through your nose and blow the air out through your mouth. Keep breathing slowly until you feel the hand over your abdomen rise and fall; otherwise, you are not breathing in deep enough. (When you are used to breathing deeply, you may skip this part.)

2. As you breathe deeply, visualize a bright white light about five feet above the top of your head, shining down on you. Feel the warmth and joy in that light radiating from its connection to the Oneness.

3. Feel the light entering through a spot on the top of your head—your crown chakra. Feel the light filling you with its brilliance; every cell, every part of your body is being saturated with the light as it travels down though your body, through your legs and your feet, and into the ground. Feel your body connected to the earth.

4. Feel your feet growing roots and sinking into the ground, deeper and deeper until you feel as if you are a part of the earth below. You are now "grounded."

5. Next, visualize that white light flowing in all directions from your pores. See it in your mind's eye, encircling you, below and above you, traveling in a clockwise direction. You are now in a cocoon of white light. Let it grow and expand to whatever size you want. Let it fill a room, a house, a city, or whatever else you may need.

If you have never put a white light shield around yourself to protect against negative energies, you may be attracting them. On occasion, these entities attach themselves to people and act like invisible energy vampires, draining their victim. This draining can happen when you are full of anger, hate, fear, envy, or other negative emotions that these negative spirits feed on. Those who are addicted to alcohol and drugs may also attract them because generally these are not happy individuals. Through their attachment to living beings, astral realm residents can influence people to do negative things they would not normally do.

If you ever feel an attachment from the astral realm, simply tell the entity to go away and never come back. Let it know that it does not belong in this plane of existence and you do not want it around. However, you may also want to consult a psychic or someone else who works with such spirits to give you further guidance.

A Dark Entity Experience

On one occasion after I had done energy clearing work for a client, I kept seeing a dark energy entity hanging around. It felt angry and full of negativity. The entity was tall, masculine, and somewhat physically attractive in a menacing sort of way. The face was human but not totally so. The entity was trying to attach to my energy field, but it was not able to hold on because I have a large, strong field and project love to others around me. Every time I shut my eyes, I could see him and feel his presence. At first it startled me, but then I remembered I was the one who had the power because I was physically alive and he was in spirit form only.

I murmured to myself, "If I have anything to say, you're not about to get any closer." Out loud I said, "Go away and never come back because I represent the light and you do not belong anywhere near me."

That was nine years ago, and I have not been bothered by this entity since.

However, as I write this book, I see and feel spirits around me. I have even felt some feather-light touches on my hands and arms as they rest on the keyboard. These particular spirits and guides are here to help and encourage me, as well as give information. Thank you, spirits and guides.

A Wake-Up Call!

Shield yourself, be aware of what is around you, and stay in an emotional state of love and gratitude. These precautions will help protect you from negative energies and bring you joy.

CHAPTER 13

Reincarnation

The world is round and the plans which seem like the end may also be only the beginning.

—Ivy Baker

The Council states,

> When rewriting the Christian Bible, the Council of Constantinople eliminated the concept of reincarnation. The religious leaders wanted to have more control over their congregations instead of letting people know that they would have many more chances to correct their mistakes during future lives. When one makes a choice in life, it does not necessarily end there, although humans may want it to end there.
>
> On Earth, human souls are trapped in a cycle of birth and death. These souls return into the physical world of suffering

until they make a choice to reconnect with God. That is why humankind keeps experiencing the war between light and shadow. Civilizations have come and gone, and still the battle continues. However, at this time, humanity is in the final chapter of this age-old conflict.

I have experienced a number of dreams, visions, and intuitive knowledge concerning some of my former lives. I have also had other psychics tell me about other previous lifetimes.

One of my most surprising past-life insights came as I was sitting on the couch, watching *The Little Mermaid* with my granddaughter. The video showed Ariel, the mermaid, jumping into the ocean from a high rock. As she jumped, I had a flash of myself being thrown out of a tower into the ocean to drown. I felt three sets of men's hands on my body and arms. I also experienced the emotional terror as I went over the stone balustrade. All in a split-second recall.

This vision related to a former life in Europe, where I was supposed to be the successor to the throne, but my jealous sibling had convinced others to dispose of me so she could be the successor. I knew this instinctively as the vision flashed into my mind. However, more detailed identification like the specific country and date were not included.

Other insights have spontaneously come in vivid dreams that seemed like reality. Those dreams always stay imprinted in my mind with great color and clarity. The intuitive knowledge associated with these dreams and visions are usually detailed and extensive.

In one such dream I was the captured male leader in one of two warring tribes. I was being held in an ancient Viking stone dungeon built on a cliff next to the sea. Through my little barred window I could see a large ship with massive sails working its way into the harbor. I knew it was coming to save me, but it would be too late. My execution was to be carried out scant minutes before my rescuers could reach me.

Some of these spontaneous glimpses into my past lives have spurred me to actively work on gaining more information through soul journeys. The shamanic soul journey is an ancient spiritual practice used to connect with alternative reality to gain information. On these journeys, I have repeatedly found myself as a Native American medicine woman.

In one lifetime I had a live bear as my helper and companion, but an enemy of our tribe killed my bear. I was devastated in my grief. My husband (he's my husband again in this lifetime) skinned my fallen bear and preserved the hide. I always kept the treasured bearskin with me, and my bear companion kept working with me from the spirit realm. My intuition tells me that this same bear energy has been associated with me in multiple lifetimes. During that particular lifetime, the bear had incarnated to actively participate in the same physical lifetime with me.

In this current lifetime I also work with the bear, among other animals. My medicine staff has a bear's head. When I received this medicine staff as a Christmas present from a friend, I immediately felt the bear spirit from that former life coming back to once again assist me.

Experiencing prior life insights is often like being a simultaneous observer and a participant of the event. An interesting observation is that many of these insights have concerned my death in former lives. This truly confirms for me that reincarnation is a fact.

Upon death, humans cast off their physical bodies. But death is not the end. Death is only a transition to a different dimension of existence. Jung wrote that our soul becomes our spirits upon death, and that our souls do not die because they are immortal. All my guides and the Star Council of Light agree with that statement.

After physical death, a spirit who has chosen the light cannot stay in the physical realm for long without a body. Unless we have learned all the lessons our souls need to reach a higher consciousness level and return to the Oneness, after death we reincarnate into yet another body. In this way, humans continue to make life purpose contracts to learn and grow over multiple lifetimes.

A Wake-Up Call!

Birth was a change of dimensions, and death is only a change back to where our spirits came from, the Oneness. The physical bodies we assume during this lifetime are to help us learn specific lessons to increase conscious awareness, to become more perfect in unconditional love and compassion for others, and to live in balance with All That Is. In this way, we become more perfect, more like the part of the Creator that we really are. All the problems we face in our lifetimes are designed to help us understand what we need to change to live by the Codes of Life.

CHAPTER 14

Walk-Ins and Other Worlds of Existence

Millions of spiritual creatures walk the earth Unseen, both when we wake and when we sleep.

—John Milton, *Paradise Lost*

A Shocking Experience

I was just beginning to go to sleep one night when I experienced a vision/dream. I was on another world, which I knew was not Earth. A large black animal about the size of a lion was coming toward me at an angle from my left. I was fascinated, and fear rooted me to where I stood. The animal projected immense power, and I was afraid he was going to harm me. But at the same time, I felt such a strong connection to him that it almost felt like he was a part of me.

He had a shiny, jet-black, leathery face similar to that of a gorilla. The rest of him was covered in long black ringlets of hair. His tail was like a whip, shiny black leather with only the tip sprouting those same black ringlets. He was majestic and dramatically beautiful to behold.

Then I noticed he was part of a pack of about ten animals. They all looked just like him, but they were walking slightly ahead of him. As they drew closer, my fear increased. I stood petrified yet fascinated. The animal pack passed by without even glancing in my direction. I intuitively knew that the solitary animal I first saw was the leader of the pack even though he was walking behind the others. After they all left, I felt a sense of deep loss.

As I became fully aware of my surroundings, my mind was full of unanswered questions: Where had I been? Who were these beautiful, fearsome creatures? Why did I feel such a connection to the leader?

Information from Spirit often comes in bits and pieces. Sometimes it feels like I'm putting together a jigsaw puzzle with several pieces missing. Patience always rewards me with more information eventually.

A few weeks later, my husband Kirk and I were en route to a local animal shelter to return a cat carrier we had borrowed when we brought home our new Lynx Point Siamese cat, Mooshie. We decided to go and "just look" at the other cats, still caged and hopefully waiting for new homes.

In one of the cages I spotted a tiny, dirty, scrawny, pale gray bundle of fur with a few spots of orange and brown on her head. The shade of gray was unusual, and the little stray had been named Smoky. She had been found wandering the street as a homeless cat. Of course we had to see this little creature. Because she looked so pathetic, our hearts went out to her. At first she was terrified and tried to hide, but we petted and cuddled her before sending her back to her cage.

On the way home, I commented, "Wasn't Smoky really sweet? But there is practically nothing to her. She's so skinny. I bet she would not have survived much longer out on her own."

"I feel bad for her, too," my husband said.

"I wish we could have adopted her. She needs lots of love," I continued.

"Do you think our other two cats would accept her?" Kirk wondered aloud.

Being a sucker for animals, that question was all I needed to start urging Kirk to turn around and head back for our new little friend.

Smoky blended in well with Mooshie and Wolfie, our long-haired tabby tomcat. Smoky was the size of a half-grown kitten. Our other two felines gave her a cool reception, but she just made herself at home anyway. The three of them got on well—no fighting or even hissing. Mooshie and Smoky even slept together at times.

However, we had promised the shelter that we would bring Smoky back to them to be spayed as soon as she grew more stable. All my instincts told me to avoid spaying, but we had promised. So I took her in for the surgery a couple of weeks later. That evening when I picked her up after the operation, her energy seemed very different, as if she'd had a very bad day, but that was understandable. That evening we put her in a spare bedroom to recover peacefully. The next morning, the day after her surgery, we brought Smoky out of the bedroom to rejoin our family. We were in for the surprise of our lives as another piece of the puzzle from my dream fell into place.

Smoky was sitting on a low kitchen counter when Wolfie walked by. Smoky let out a growl that belonged to a lion, not a little post-surgery cat. She took off like a streak, chasing poor Wolfie. This post-surgery cat (who was not supposed to jump or do any major exercise in order to protect her stitches) was not acting like her former self at all. She ran so fast that I could not react quickly enough to catch her as she dashed through my hands. Both Mooshie and Wolfie hid until I put Smoky back in the bedroom. We thought this personality change might be due to a bad reaction to the anesthesia and it would wear off in a few days.

After five more days, Smoky was still acting like a predator, howling and going on the offensive, in attack mode each time she saw one of the other cats. I did some energy work on her, sending healing light energy into her system to raise her vibration, clearing any blockages and enhancing Smoky's mental and physical healing. I also put Bach Flower Essences® into her food and water to create emotional balance. The flower essences I used include following:

- Walnut to help Smoky deal with the change.
- Vine to mellow her strong-willed and domineering behavior.
- Holly and Willow to counteract her possible envy, anger, jealousy, and resentment.
- Star of Bethlehem to help her deal with the surgery trauma.
- Rescue Remedy for general stress relief.

Nothing helped. Smoky's unacceptable behavior toward the other cats continued. The animal shelter's behavior specialists were not able to come up with any solutions either. After two weeks post surgery, Smoky continued to be cuddly and loving toward my husband and me but kept attacking the cats on sight. We had to keep Smoky secluded, which she seemed to resent.

We were at our wits' end because both of us were really attached to her by now. I decided to get external help. I asked my friend Pam Storrs, a hypno-therapist, medium, medical intuitive, and animal communicator, to "talk" to Smoky and help us find out what was going on.

During the session, Smoky informed Pam that she was sharing her body with the spirit of another animal, the big black creature I had seen in my dream/vision. In other words, we now had a cat that was hosting a *walk-in*. Walk-ins are spirits that take over another's physical body with permission of the original owner, who wants to end his or her life. This is a reasonably rare occurrence. Unbelievable! It shocked me that this could happen to a cat—especially my cat. Neither Pam nor I had ever heard of an animal walk-in before. After further discussion, we named the walk-in spirit, Disco.

Through Pam, Disco told us of himself.

He'd "had his eye" on Smoky because he knew we were going to adopt her, and she was a way for him to reconnect with me. Smoky had allowed him to share her body. Smoky's and Disco's spirits were both in that minuscule cat body. Disco explained that he was not attacking the other cats to harm them but to simply get them to be submissive to him.

In a former life, he and I had been on another planet called Zandu, where we had worked together to help that planet's residents during a time of crisis. His spirit had come back to work with me again in this lifetime on Earth.

Disco would not agree to leave the other cats alone or stop attacking them. His statement to Pam was, "I cannot do that. It is not in my nature to ignore their lack of respect and acceptance of me as their leader."

When given the option of going back to the shelter or quit chasing and frightening the other cats, he willingly chose to go back to the shelter. His final words were, "I will return when the other two cats are no longer living."

It was a painful parting. Kirk and I both shed tears. Disco, however, went into his cage at the shelter and immediately started to eat, ignoring us. We still miss Smoky/Disco. But we often see and feel the paws of an invisible "phantom cat" in the house, and intuitively I know Disco is still connected to us.

Another piece of the same puzzle came a couple of years later still as I attended a group past-life regression session with Dick Suthpen. Our assignment was to go to a past life that had some connection to our present one.

During the session I found myself in a spaceship traveling to Zandu, the same planet Disco had claimed to be from. As I landed on Zandu, it felt like I had come home. I experienced a deep feeling of love and welcome. My body looked different from its present appearance. I was still a biped but very tall, maybe ten feet or so, and thin with limbs like those of a praying mantis. I had lots of black hair, which was worn in a knot on top of my head. My face was similar to a human's yet different, long and narrow with sunken cheeks.

This incident served for me as additional proof that life exists in many other places, many other dimensions and realms of reality. Earth is not the only place in the Universe that hosts life, but Earth is the only place where spirit comes to make the choice of connecting to the light or to the darkness. The Smoky/Disco incident is not the only experience I have had with visitors from other planets.

Visitors

Many visitors have come to this planet throughout its history. Numerous light workers have seen and/or interacted with aliens. A majority of these other-world beings have come to help humanity. The Pleiadians are one group of aliens who have come to Earth in physical bodies to help humanity with evolution into more light. The Pleiadians have been written about by many authors, including Barbara Marciniak in her books *Bringers of the Dawn*, *Family of Light*, and *Earth: Pleiadian Keys to the Living Library*. Another author, Barbara Hand Clow, has written the *Pleiadian Agenda*.

In addition to the aliens who are here to help humanity, there are others from the shadow side who bring negative energy vibrations that create disruptions. One can recognize some of the shadow-based entities by the emptiness in their eyes. Their eyes have no depth reflection of the soul within because they do not have souls. If one is sensitive, one can feel the emotional coldness coming from them. These beings feel no compassion, guilt, or true ability to love, but they are good at faking it if it is to their advantage.

Spirit tells me,

> *Alien beings known as the* grays, *are walking on the streets with you.* [These are the ones with large oval eyes that are depicted as the aliens in the UFO crash in Roswell, New Mexico, several decades ago.] *Many of these aliens may sound like normal human beings, but do not trust or believe them. They are here to take power and control. The grays do not have souls like the light beings. Grays, however, have the ability to shape-shift, so they can appear as human or appear to be a spirit guide in order to get people to trust and believe them. Do not cultivate a relationship with them. They are the beings who do cattle mutilations and abductions. Humans who worship Satan and do satanic rituals are also mutilating cattle. The grays have taught them how to do these things. None of these behaviors are of the light.*

A Wake-Up Call!

There are amazing new wonders in the Universe beyond the limits of human experience. Life is an ongoing wonder, and it is exciting to see what the next steps hold. Staying open to the possibilities is important.

CHAPTER 15

Spirit Guides and Animal Messages

I like pigs. Dogs look up to us. Cats look down on us. Pigs treat us as equals.

—Winston Churchill

Meeting your spirit guide(s) is a spiritual journey, not a mental process. Since there are several good books by Ted Andrews and Sylvia Browne, among others, on how-to techniques for meeting and working with your guides, it will not be covered in this book.

However, keep in mind that communicating with your guide(s) can be confusing at first. Spirit guides are a consciousness that is not physical and may communicate with you telepathically by projecting thoughts or visual images. These messages can feel like your imagination or daydreams, but often this is how the communication comes through. Spirit guides may also communicate by using any of your senses, including the use of colors. Do not carry any preconceived expectation about the process because there is a wide range of variances. It depends on each person's abilities and the guide you are working with.

One important thing to remember when working with spirit guides is that the information you get is not time specific because the time line we use does not exist in their dimension. Also, based on Earth events and your personal choices, things can change moment to moment. Reality is not a hard and fast absolute. In addition, never tell anyone bad news based on a message you get from your spirit guides; it is not ethical and can be destructive for the individual receiving the message. Always look for a way to phrase things from a positive perspective.

Animal Energies and Wisdom

According to Spirit,

> *Animals are teachers and guides who can bring warnings and knowledge. They are the ones to look for when seeking the light. Every animal has a certain energy or vibration that embodies the spirit of their particular lesson and information about that lesson. Animal energies are connected to nature, so they can sense if there is any possible danger. Animals know the best way to stay safe.*

When the tsunami hit Indonesia after an ocean earthquake in 2006, related news articles discussed how prior to the actual wall of water hitting the shore, the elephants screamed and broke their chains to escape to higher ground. Many indigenous natives also deserted their homes to climb to higher ground. If everyone had observed the animals and followed their behaviors, there would have been far fewer deaths.

Spirit tells me,

Animals are not more intelligent than humans. However, they may be wiser in some sense because they are connected to the natural order of life. The animals with the greatest sense of the natural life order are the most intelligent ones. Some of these more intelligent creatures are from the sea and include dolphins and whales. Some birds of prey are also intelligent, but not to the level of dolphins or whales.

Mammals in the canine family and its close relation, such as the wolf, are also intelligent. Cats are generally smarter than some dogs because cats act on instinctual wisdom while dogs react according to learned behavior, in the Pavlovian sense. Cheetahs also have a higher intelligence while domestic pigs are smarter than horses or cats.

Owls are known as the birds of wisdom because they are awake in the evening and have their eyes wide open at night. So symbolically they are awake even in the dark, which is where the general concept of their wisdom is derived.

Some animals are evening creatures while others are more active during the day. Each animal represents an important opportunity to understand and learn about life. If you are willing to allow animals to come into your life, call them. They will bring valuable lessons with them.

Spirit continues,

Each person has a personal animal spirit guide—sometimes more than one. If a specific lesson is necessary at a particular time, an animal will bring that message. The animals that come to you in a dream or ones that keep appearing during your daily routine are the ones whose lessons you need to explore. Learn what lesson each animal represents. It's very important for your personal spiritual growth.

Whether you have a personal connection to an animal or not, all animals provide lessons that humans can learn simply by observing them. Such lessons can be found in the manner in which animals live and behave. Follow, observe, and as you watch, you can learn many things from any animal you are attracted to. However, remember that some animals carry poison for protection against predators. If humans intrude on these creatures, they will protect themselves. So use caution.

North American Animals and Their Lessons

Spirit advises that the following are important animals to observe for their lessons. There are many other animals, birds, and reptiles with valuable lessons, but these are connected to this point in time.

Ant—Builder, Minute Awareness, Working in Community
This is a reminder not to make a mountain out of an anthill. The ant works on building a system. Although small, the ant accomplishes a lot. The ant's size seems to indicate that it offers a very small message, but in actuality, the message is of significant importance. The ant sees itself as part of a whole team and works on doing its part unconditionally.

Do you think you are small and insignificant? You are not.

Bat—Rebirth.
The bat carries the dual energies of the light and darkness—the shape shifter, the shadow. The bat has the ability to transmute energy

of the lower frequency into a higher one through the use of ceremony. Bats can remind us when we need to do ceremony or that it's time to transition to a new way of thinking or acting.

Is the bat telling you that a change needs to happen in your life or that a new way of approaching something or of thinking is needed?

Bear—Insight, Strength, Perseverance

To have insight and clarity, one must persevere. The bear also represents the connection to the inner-self, going within oneself in the same manner as the bear goes into the cave to hibernate. Bear is good at hibernating, but it can also defend when necessary. As the bear transforms into the energy of the warrior, it stands on two legs instead of four. Bear holds the blueprint of taking an idea into the practical. They know how to withdraw, to regenerate, and then to emerge and do what is needed. Bears are most fierce when seeking food or protecting their young. Bear is attracted to sweet things like honey, which represents the sweet things in life. Do not be overly attracted to what appears sweet on the outside. Instead, look for what is on the inside and gain an intricate awareness of its motivation.

Are you distracted by the sweet things of life? Do you meditate and go inside to regenerate, or are you acting like a warrior to defend something? If bear is speaking to you, what is the lesson?

Buffalo—Prayer, the World, Wisdom of the Sacred Path

The buffalo is known for the sacrifice of giving his all. When the Native hunters killed a buffalo, every piece of his body was used in some way. Absolutely nothing was wasted. The buffalo represents the world and prayer. He is walking on the Red Road, the spiritual path. As Native Americans followed this pathway, they were led to sacred places for their ceremonies. The buffalo's four legs represent the four directions of the world—north, south, east, and west.

The Sioux tell the story of the White Buffalo Calf Woman and her teachings about lifestyle, ceremonies, and prayer. She taught them seven ceremonies to perform to keep positive energy flowing. Seven because there are seven sacred directions—east, west, north, south, above, below, and within. The ceremonies she gave them are the sweat lodge; the sun dance; the vision quest; the making of relatives; the keeping of the soul; preparing a girl for womanhood; and the throwing of the ball. Then she promised to come back when the end times were near.

Is the buffalo telling you that you need to do more sacrifice? Are you walking the Red Road of Spirituality with compassion, gratitude, and service to those in need?

Butterfly—Ascension, Transformation, Transcendence

The butterfly goes through very visible stages of growth. It has the ability to shift from its physically denser caterpillar stage to going within the cocoon and ultimately transforming to light of spirit. This change is called ascension because it moves up the scale to a higher vibration. The message of the butterfly is the metamorphosis, the movement from the denser form into the light.

If the butterfly lands in your life, consider your personal transformation progress and consider which stage you are in at present. Are you still the caterpillar in the cocoon, or are you unfolding your wings in preparation of flight?

Cat—Dark, Spirit Watchers

The cat is connected to the dream time, when you are sleeping and your spirit is out of the physical body, reconnected to the Universe in circular time. Their dream time connection makes them part of the visioning energy. They can see at night, in the dark, or in near dark. They can also see spirits. Cats walk very lightly so others cannot hear them, and they land on their feet in times of trouble. The cat can help you to tread carefully in difficult times.

Is this a message for you to take things more lightly and pay more attention to your dreams?

Coyote—Trickster, Humorous

With the coyote's trickster energy, all isn't as it appears to be. Yet a coyote is not deceptive. One of coyote's messages is not to take everything so seriously, to laugh at your own mistakes. He also brings the message of caution, of being careful and using all your resources, because this world can be deceptive. He follows the wolves as a scavenger and watches them very carefully. Humans can also turn into scavengers if survival is at stake.

The lesson of the coyote is to be proud of what you have. He would like to be a wolf and carry that dignity or to be as fast as a fox, but he isn't. So learn about justice and fairness through the positive resources you already have.

Be proud of who you are, and don't worry about your mistakes. Mistakes are how you learn. Remember to play and laugh.

Crow—Spiritual Law

The crow uses the repetition of his *caw, caw, caw* to remind us of Spiritual Law and to obey it. The message from crows is loud and repetitive because mankind needs to remember and hear it over and over again.

Is the crow reminding you of the law, or is it confirming you are on the right path?

Deer—Gentleness, Kindness

The deer is connected to the heart. They employ grace and lightness to move through all of life's situations. Deer need to be fast and to be aware at all times, even when sleeping. Yet they do this in a peaceful, gentle way and are not fearful. They maintain kind, gentle energy even when they know that many larger species hunt and want to eat them. The gentle energy of the deer can often overcome obstacles that even brute strength can't move.

Are you facing your gentle side toward others and yourself, especially toward yourself?

Dog—Trust, Loyalty

Dog represents trust even in the face of adversity. Its strength is different from the other animals because the dog also brings a message of dependability that we can rely on when we need help and support from others. In a relationship, the dog protects us and watches over us. A dog chases away negative spirits from the astral dimension.

Are you trusting too much or not enough?

Dolphin—Harmonics, the Vibration of Life

The dolphin represents sound, the harmonics, and cycles of the seasons, which are like the Circle of Life (birth, youth, adulthood, and old age). The harmonics will guide you and help you find protection through the vibration of sound. Harmonics teach you to stay in the flow of nature/life and to enjoy the "seasons" and all they bring.

The dolphin also represents the birth-womb because of its ability to communicate from the subtle energy of intention. The subtle energy is being broadcast on the spiritual level, so it can be sensed/heard in the physical realm to help you raise your consciousness.

Are you paying attention and staying in the flow, or does your intention need fine tuning?

Eagle—Wisdom, Spiritual Overview, Prayer

Because eagle can fly so high, it takes prayers to the Great Spirit. It represents the voice and connection with Spirit. The eagle comes when there is going to be a ceremony of some sort. It can give you the sign that you are on the right track.

Is eagle taking your prayers to the Great Spirit on a regular basis?

Fox—Cleverness

The message of the fox is to go in the back way instead of coming at things directly. The way of the fox is the ability to be subtle and to say what needs to be said in an indirect manner. Fox can get out of bad situations very quickly and easily because of its cleverness. Do not take things at face value, because what is real may be hidden beneath the surface. Look inward instead of outward.

Are there situations in your life that need the more subtle touch of fox energy?

Frog—Cleansing, Creative

The frog is connected to the cleansing properties of water. A frog is acutely emotional, and its jumping energy always needs to move, to jump out of something. It may be telling you to move out of the way of a danger that is coming toward you and to use your creative energy to do it. Its repetitive croak is connected to the need for things to be repeated.

If a frog comes to you, consider what needs "cleansing."

Grasshopper—Preparation, Jumping

Grasshopper's jumping energy is different from the frog's because it is connected to the earth and the sky. Its message tells you to prepare and be ready for whatever is to come. The grasshopper carries a busy energy. Like the locust, it moves quickly, swirling in a circular fashion.

Could its message be that you are moving too quickly and you need to have more focus and clarity? Or maybe you're just too busy and need to take some time for you? It is important to always take care of yourself, never forgetting your own journey in life.

Hawk—Sharpness, Clarity of Vision

The hawk sees the details but in a different way than the fox, for the hawk implies an image of laserlike sharpness. In addition, it can see things at a distance, so it can see things coming. The hawk tells you to rise above the situation so you can see it clearly.

Are you using hawk's message to see things from a bigger picture perspective?

Horse—Ability, Power

The horse has the ability to rise to adversity by rearing on it hind legs. Its message is that you can face challenges with power and strength. You can help and support others just as the horse can carry someone on his back while traveling long distances. To use the positive energy of the horse, you need to be focused. Otherwise, the energy could become that of the wild horse, which could be negative and destructive.

Horse and eagle can work together because an eagle represents sky energy and horse implies the power of the earth. This brings together the "above" and the "below" to create a whole.

How are you reacting to challenges? Do you need to be more focused?

Mouse—Detail

The mouse is very small and connected to the essence of each situation. When it speaks, it speaks very softly, so you have to listen closely and pay attention to both the subtle and overt messages.

The mouse used to be much larger and was overbearing in its behavior. Spirit taught the mouse a lesson by making it very small with a small voice so it would only speak those things that were meaningful. When the mouse was big, it did not have a tail. The ancient mouse had a tendency to not pay attention to anything but the obvious. A modern example would be seeing the cheese in the mousetrap without seeing the trap's spring. The tail was a reminder to be smarter and stay out of situations that could trap it, because the tail is so easy to grab.

Is there a situation to which you need to pay more attention?

Pig—Intelligence, Self-Esteem

Appearance can be deceiving. Pigs' nature in ancient times was to be vain, and therefore a lesson of humility was necessary. Spirit put the pig in its present body to learn a life lesson. The pig has to roll in the mud to stay cool, but in doing so, it becomes smelly and messy. As a result, its intelligence is not obvious.

The lesson of the pig is that there are two kinds of dirt—internal and external. Mud, on the outside, is only physical dirt that can be washed off. Vanity, on the other hand, makes one dirty on the inside, and that kind of soiling does not wash off. The lesson is also of self-esteem based on whom you are, not what you look like.

Are you overly concerned with your image?

Rabbit—Awareness, Fear

The rabbit spends much of his time being afraid, even when there is nothing to be afraid of. So its destiny is to live much of its life underground. Energetically, what rabbit signifies isn't fear as we know fear; rather it's an awareness of one's environment. The rabbit's message is not to tell everything you know but to express it only when necessary or to make your stand.

Spirit tells us that originally the rabbit did not have the big ears it now has. The ears were very small. Rabbit's message was still the same one of increased awareness, but rabbit was not very aware. So Spirit gave him big ears as a reminder to listen.

Do you live with fear as your companion? Maybe rabbit is telling you to be more aware and look for ways to overcome the fear by having an action plan for coping if the worst were to happen.

Raven—Magic, Builder

The raven's magic is the shape-shifting energy. The magic comes from his knowledge of how to use elemental law and the energies of water, wind, earth, and fire. Raven understands those energies and so is able to focus his intention to use their energy. The lesson is about learning to focus your intention on the desired outcome. This is another version of the law of attraction.

Have you focused on what you really want, really focused, not just wished for? Make a vision board and put it where you see it all the time to stimulate your focus.

Raccoon—Curiosity

The raccoon has to gather the information in such a way that it can open previously closed areas and then remove information that had been locked away. The lesson tells us to explore and honor your curiosity. Only by exploring the unknown can you grow in wisdom and progress

What have you done to satisfy your curiosity?

Snake—Karma, Discernment

Long ago, the snake had legs instead of having to slither on the ground. The snake had legs so he could carry a warning message that someone or some situation was not what it appeared. But the snake did not carry the warning, so it lost its legs.

There are two different levels connected to the snake message. One is the positive transmutation that comes with shedding the old skin and moving onto a higher vibration. The second message is negative and relates to the message of deception.

Have you dreamed of or seen snakes lately? Don't assume the worst, but investigate.

Spider—Weaver of Life, Messenger

The spider has eight legs and can appear to be coming and going at the same time. There are many native legends about the spider. One of the tales is about the spider serving as a messenger to warn the varied Indian tribes about coming changes. The spider described the coming of the Conquistadors riding horses and wearing armor long before they actually arrived.

The spider represents manifesting and is especially helpful if you are involved with legal issues. Spider is the weaver of life patterns in its web. Its web thread is one of the strongest materials in the world, but be careful not to use the pattern before it is ready. Plan to avoid confusion just as the spider strategically weaves the web to trap his dinner.

Consider the resources and materials being used for your weaving because your life form/cloth will only be as strong as your thread. Are your threads based on love and gratitude? Or are you being given a message to share?

Squirrel—Storer, Gatherer

The squirrel could be bringing you the message that you are accumulating excess baggage. Its energy is that of spring cleaning, sorting out what is no longer needed if you have too much. But it also brings the message of gathering resources. Squirrel is aware of the need to prepare for the future. It flits about lightly and fearfully but not like the rabbit. Squirrel has a purpose of gathering food for the winter when there is none.

Excess baggage slows down your progress and holds you back like an anchor because the energy can't move smoothly. Check for mental as well as physical baggage that needs to be disposed of. Then fill the vacated space with light energy.

Turtle—Retreating, Carrying

The turtle is connected to Mother Earth. He carries the energy of support and nurturing, like the Earth Mother. The turtle also personalizes the energy of going within to retreat for protection when necessary. It represents caring for itself, for others, and for the earth. The earth needs protection now, so turtle energy is timely and important. A turtle is hard and rigid on the surface but soft inside.

Do you forget to care for yourself while taking care of others?

Whale—Record Keeper, Memory from the Beginning of Time

The whale's harmonic calls are haunting, like the echoes of all the ancient secrets stored from the beginning of time. These secrets are the recording of history of all vibrations manifested into physical form. The whale's call can also bring a foreboding of something that needs to be examined in your personal essence or at the core level from your past lives.

Have you ever meditated to the sound of the whales' calls to see what the harmonics bring up?

Wolf—Teacher, Spiritual Protection

The eyes of the wolf are intense, able to look inside. Wolf energy helps others by bringing in spiritual wisdom and teaching. Wolf energy is different from that of the dog. As a good teacher, the wolf finishes what he starts. The wolf works in a pack, mating for life, taking care of his family and his relationships with loyalty. A wolf knows where the life-path is and how to walk it by himself, but he also helps others to walk it.

If wolf energy comes to you, look to your leadership role in life. Have you stepped off the path, or are you taking full responsibility?

For more information consult such books as *Animal Speak* or *Animal Wise* by Ted Andrews and *Animal Guides* by Steven Farmer. Another excellent resource is *Medicine Cards: The Discovery of Power Through the Way of Animals* by Jamie Sams and David Carson

Many individuals can communicate with animals as children, but they seem to lose this ability as they grow up. Growing up changes their priorities, focus, and perception of reality. It is possible to recapture this ability by reactivating one's ability to accept things with an open mind to possibilities. It is also helpful to cultivate an open, receptive, compassionate, and nonjudgmental attitude with prayer and self-acceptance.

A Wake-up Call!

Animals are much more than friends and companions; they can also be our teachers and helpers if we let them. Trust their wisdom and judgment about other humans since animals are able to sense an individual's trustworthiness. This is especially true of felines. If your cat will not have anything to do with your new friend, maybe you shouldn't either.

PART 4

Action Steps for Your Life Journey

CHAPTER 16

Cleansing Storms

Oh beautiful for smoggy skies, insecticided grain,
For strip-mined mountain majesty above the asphalt plain.
America, America, man sheds his waste on thee,
And hides the pines with billboard signs, from sea to oily sea.
—George Carlin

When asked about the extensive changes in the weather worldwide, Spirit clarified what is happening:

> *The storms that humanity and the planet are experiencing represent the conflict between the growing spiritual awareness and the status quo, between the things you have always done and the manner in which you have always done them. Sometimes there is even conflict between your own conscience and the people you love. **This is the time to stand for what you believe in. Defend your own truth. The cleansing storms stand for rebellion—the***

war between the light and shadow dimensions. When people recognize that the world is all one nation, wars will cease to happen. Then mankind will experience a new age of harmony and balance.

There are many difficult times ahead for the residents of the earth. The weather disturbances, fires, hurricanes, tornadoes, and earthquakes are called the "cleansing storms." The prophecies of old from different sources all say this is the time. The earth is in the final phase, and we are about to witness the dawn of the new age. This is a time of acceleration and transformation. Changes are moving much faster now and appear very dark. In reality, dark things are happening. Presently, what is sacred is of secondary importance in the way which most people live their lives.

The Universe regularly contains different levels of negative energy. As you move forward in daily life you normally release emotional energy, both positive and negative. But when someone is purposely committing negative actions (e.g., abusing the body with drugs, stealing, behaving violently) those actions create a stronger negative energy. That negative energy then literally goes into the planet. This explains why you are experiencing the cleansing storms and earth changes. The earth has a natural way of cleansing itself when it is overloaded with negative energy. But presently, the high level of negative energy that is being generated is creating a crisis overload for the planet. Prayers can help dissipate the negative energy, but they cannot dissolve it.

The earth's ley lines are shifting. The crystalline formations are breaking down and changing beneath the earth. Such changes impact how energy is conducted through the planet and how the life force connects to the earth. The atmosphere is also affected, as is the weather and the location of bodies of water. The bodies of water have already begun to change, according to the ley line location. This is not good because the changes could result in flooding inhabited land. Entire cities could vanish beneath the sea.

The hole in the ozone layer of the earth has been worse in the past than it is now. However, the planet has always been able to heal itself before. Now there are more holes in the atmosphere than ever before. Mankind is releasing more chemicals into the atmosphere faster than ever before, faster than the earth has the ability to regenerate. So everything is out of balance. Changes in the earth's magnetic poles are causing the earth's rotation to slow down. Climates in many areas are changing, and the soil has become depleted of nutrients. It is also impacting the sea creatures such as whales, which are beaching themselves.

The shift of Earth's electromagnetic poles and of the atmospheric pressure creates movement in the oceans. This movement influences the rising tides, and the size of ocean waves become enormous. An example is the 2006 tsunami in Indonesia, which was the result of ocean-based earthquakes. In areas where strong winds are typical, hurricane-force winds will blow more frequently, especially along the Gulf Coast area from Florida to Texas.

Humankind has not been a good steward of the earth. Your practices have been destructive. The manufacturing and pharmaceutical chemicals can be found throughout the entire food chain. Earth, air, and water are all contaminated by pollutants.

Some of the disasters the planet is experiencing are the result of man's depleting activities. There has been a practice of taking things like minerals and other resources without giving anything back to the planet. So the earth is now taking back of its own accord. Some of the disasters are a part of the earth's normal cleansing, as a part of its life process. When something is old, it cleanses itself like a forest might with a fire. But much of what is happening on Earth now is a direct result of human-caused imbalances. The same imbalance is happening to the human body through stress, illness, and disease.

These problems on Earth are often caused by human ignorance and greed. The ways of the ancients should not be forgotten. Earth's ability to regenerate itself is affected by those indigenous peoples who are still performing ceremonies designed to bring light energy of the stars back to the earth (e.g., the Sioux with their Sun Dance). Earth's regeneration is connected to the human consciousness level and its ability to bring in light energy.

Humanity's higher consciousness level is growing, and a seed of light has been planted by those who are considered light workers. That seed will grow into the Tree of Life, which we discussed earlier. This tree will help humanity communicate with the stars again and rejoin the Star Nation. This tree will bear fruit and provide shelter during the storm for those who have affiliated with the light. This process is not an ending but a new beginning of harmony and balance.

As 2012 of the Mayan calendar draws closer, Spirit has verified that we really are approaching the shift of consciousness, as prophesied.

When the light and dark dimensions blend, the doorway to the spirit world opens and closes. The result is that many people are having more psychic experiences and are looking for mediums/seers to give them readings. There are more reports of alien visitations, more unidentified flying objects (UFO) sightings, etc. (Spirit calls them "identified flying objects" or IFOs.) As consciousness levels increase, many people are shifting their viewpoints and belief systems. But many people will suffer more physical imbalances if they don't allow the light to enter into their bodies as part of the Shift.

With the earth's pollution, there are too many man-made chemicals in the human bodies and in our environment. Spirit guides have advised me that we should purchase and consume products that are more helpful and healthy for our bodies. Spirit says,

> *There is no need to poison yourself by ingesting unhealthy foods and drugs, because there are already too many poisons in the atmosphere.*

A Wake-Up Call!

It is interesting to note how quickly organic foods are gaining popularity and several new health food type grocery stores are opening across the country. It's as if the universe is guiding humanity to eat better. Also available now are super-food nutrient drinks. One example is Original Limu™, which is made from pure Tongan Island seaweed to provide humanity with many of the vitamins and minerals missing in much of our food. These nutrients give our body what it needs to build the immune system and maintain improved health.

CHAPTER 17

Crystal Energies

The moment I give close attention to anything, even a blade of grass it becomes mysterious, awesome, an indescribably magnificent world in itself.

—Henry Miller

The information in this section covers only the primary crystals that I have been guided to use and that are the most helpful at this time of the Shift. However, this is a very small percentage of all the wonderful stones available on the planet and whose energy is needed to help with the current cycle.

Spirit says,

> *Crystals are a solid form of light, a seed that was planted on Earth by the Creator. The crystal seeds, like the seed that is your soul, grow and evolve. Crystals are the light from the stars brought to Earth to bring light energy directly into the planet. They are naturally infused with light, so people*

can connect directly to them to have their own personal star links.

If you are attracted to a particular crystal when you see it and it feels harmonious to you, it might be advantageous to buy it. It has been my experience that your body will automatically be attracted to the particular crystal energies it needs. In essence, the crystals select you, not the other way around. However, if you are not sensitive to their energies, consider asking someone who knows about their qualities. Or you could consult one of the many crystal books available to find what crystals have which properties.

The following stones carry the highest vibrations to help create balance and harmony.

Amber started as the sap of an evergreen tree, so it creates a connection to the earth and the sun by its appearance, like a drop of solid sunshine. Amber is about 50 million years old and has the ability to help the body heal itself by transmuting negative energy to positive. *Copal* looks like amber and is often called by the same name, but it is sap from the copal tree and carries a younger, less intense energy.

Amethyst is a stone of spirituality and contentment. It can transmute low energy vibration to a higher vibration level. It is wonderful to use for meditation.

Chrysocolla is helpful in creating abundance. It is a combination of turquoise and malachite, so it has the energy of both stones. This stone needs periodic cleansing because the turquoise readily absorbs negative energy. Chrysocolla is a particularly helpful stone to have if one has lots of issues concerning abundance and psychological trauma about receiving money. The abundance, or lack of it, can also be of a spiritual nature. If you are having a difficult time moving through issues and you are not really open to receiving spiritual information, chrysocolla would be helpful.

Citrine is one of the few stones that never needs cleansing. It represents financial abundance. Citrine has a higher energy vibration that is helpful with intellectual stimulation and physical enhancement. It can also help foster emotional balance.

Clear Qquartz is considered a basic crystal/master stone because many other stones evolve from it. It is helpful for everyone to have a clear quartz crystal in their possession. If you cannot find a particular type of stone, the clear quartz can be used as a substitute. Clear quartz can also be used with other stones when placing stones on the body for healing purposes. It acts like a laser and represents strong energy of intense purity. If you use it with an amethyst, the clear quartz can intensify the spiritual energy of the amethyst and help move the energy through a person's body to help with balancing. When you seek energy because you are feeling drained, clear quartz can help. If you are going through an emotionally difficult time, use the clear quartz together with another stone of your choice. Using it alone can magnify the emotional energy state.

Fluorite, particularly the Chinese fluorite, which comes in a wide range of intermixed colors, ranges primarily from a deep purple to clear, turquoise, and green, among other colors. It is considered one of the most beautiful but fragile stones. The natural fracture lines in the stone represent the injuries we often carry in our psyche. Fluorite helps clear trauma, old issues, and emotional blockages from the solar plexus.

Garnet quickens the energy of whatever stone it is used with. If there is a blockage in one of the chakras, you can use garnet together with whichever other stones are appropriate to unblock it.

Herkimer Diamond can help you attune to another person, to strengthen the relationship, and to get a fresh start again. It stimulates clairvoyant, clairaudient, and telepathic capabilities.

Kyenite can dispel negative energy. It never needs to be cleansed, so it's a good stone to carry with you. Place it above doorways to help screen out anger and frustration while attracting tranquility. Kyenite can also help align the chakras discussed in chapter 9.

Lapis Lazuli aids in communication, especially verbal discourse. It has been called the stone of total awareness because it helps you to understand the messages received in the dream state. Lapis also serves as a good protection stone.

Malachite is used for focusing on abundance and prosperity. It brings in energy to heal the blocks to abundance and prosperity. This stone aids in clearing and activating all the chakras. DNA and the immune system can be regulated and enhanced with the use of malachite.

Obsidian is excellent for grounding because it connects the human spine with the heart of the earth. It is also a good protection stone that can transform and disperse negative vibrations. Obsidian can help you discover your flaws and help you understand what needs to be done to eliminate those flaws.

Rose Qquartz is an important crystal that everyone should have. It represents unconditional love and the heart. It would be beneficial to have a heart-shaped rose quartz stone to carry with you or wear regularly. However, it needs to be taken off at night to give your body a break from the enhanced energy.

Rubelite is pink tourmaline, another beneficial healing stone. It releases old negative energy patterns from one's former lives when such patterns are firmly rooted within.

Smoky Qquartz will help ground your energy. It is connected to the earth and allows you to understand who you are and where you are going in life.

Sodalite facilitates meditation and can be helpful when connecting to your spirit guide. Sodalite also helps to open the throat chakra for enhanced communication.

Tourmaline comes in varied colors, but black is the primary color found. It serves to align the left and right sides of the brain and enhance its ability to function fully. Tourmaline is also useful for grounding and transmuting negative energy to bring about increased self-confidence.

Turquoise absorbs negative energy but needs much cleansing if you use it or wear it frequently. This stone strengthens and aligns the chakras. In deep meditation, turquoise helps ground you to the conscious. It heals the spirit and is used extensively in jewelry made by the Native Americans of the Southwest.

My personal experience with turquoise has been quite positive. I was able to overcome both sinus problems and migraine headaches with its continued use.

These crystals work together and are harmonious, important factors, particularly during this time of transition to higher consciousness. Not all stones are harmonious, but it does not mean that there is anything wrong with those crystals. However, unless you are sensitive to the energy of stones and know when to bring them into your energy field, some stones can be disruptive to particular individuals. There are also certain stones that are not balanced and should not be carried on your person. Stones such as opals may actually create an imbalance in your energy field if they are with you all the time.

Follow your own heart about what stones and which corresponding qualities you want to bring into your life. Realize that a few crystals connect into the astral energy. Be conscious of what you are choosing.

Mochi Balls are an example of ones that connect to the astral realm. These stones do not have a high enough vibration to be helpful at this time. Mochi Balls were placed on the earth by the Grays as a distracting factor from humanity's consciousness evolution. Hematite is another stone that can lower your energy; unless you are of very high energy or are hyper, I do not recommend it.

Cleansing Crystals

Crystals need periodic cleansing because they absorb the energies from their environment. When a stone is exposed to intense emotional energy or becomes saturated with negative energy, the crystal can break apart. A client once related a story about how the amethyst pendant around her neck cracked and fell apart as she was having an angry argument with her husband. The fracturing or breakage is not dangerous but something to keep in mind when working with crystals. Frequency of cleansing varies, but it is useful to do it a couple times a month. More cleansing may be needed if an item is used consistently. If stones are used for healing purposes, cleanse after each use.

There are a number of effective ways to cleanse crystals. However, Spirit advises against soaking crystals in salt water because that can create holes in their energy fields. Besides, crystals such as selenite will start to melt in water while others could come apart because long-dried mud may be holding some portion of stone cluster together.

I have found that cleansing stones by smudging with white sage works the best. White sage has a higher energy vibration than other types of sage and consequently is more helpful. Some individuals prefer smudging with other herbs, a process that works well also. Smudging is a practice long used by a wide range of indigenous tribes for cleansing before ceremonies or other spiritual work. If only cleansing a small object, I find it useful and economical to only use a sage leaf or one individual stick from a sage wand.

Smudging is a way of using sage (or a similar herb) to cleanse energy. To smudge, take a sage wand or sage cluster and light the end with a match, letting it burn for a short time to build a good smoldering ember before you blow out the flame. After blowing out the flame, fan the smoke from the ember (this is the smudge) with a feather or your hand over the crystals to be cleansed. Move the sage wand in a clockwise direction as you smudge. If the ember goes out, relight it as often as necessary. The burning ember will often drop sparks; catch those sparks by holding a shell or other fireproof container underneath the smoking wand. You do not want the sparks to drop on the floor or to accidentally burn you. When finished smudging, tamp out the ember on your shell or other fireproof container to extinguish the ember. It is best to not mix the energy of fire and water by running water over the still-smoldering sage ember as a way of putting it out. When you are sure the ember is totally out, store the sage wand in a brown paper or plastic bag for future use.

Some other useful cleansing methods are also effective:
1. Crystals can be rinsed under running water and then carefully dried off.
2. Another way to cleanse and charge your stones is by placing them overnight on a clear quartz cluster.
3. You can place your crystals in the sunshine, but be careful that you don't leave them for too long, as the strong energy of the sun will bleach them. A couple of hours is sufficient. Also, be careful not to display your stones in the bright direct sunlight such as a window ledge or outside on the deck. Most will lose the majority of their color.

4. Crystals can also be buried in the earth for cleansing, but this method takes more time. A general practice is to leave them from one new moon until the next.

5. Burying your stones in sea salt is a common cleansing practice. My stones do not seem to like it as well.

6. A final way that I have been taught by my elders and spirit guides is one of blowing the intention of clearing onto the item to be cleansed. This is a practical way because nothing external is necessary. Take a couple of deep breaths and ground yourself, fill your mind with thoughts and a vision of cleansing all pollution and negative energy off the crystals, and then, blowing through your nostrils, blow three puffs of air onto the stone. That's it.

There are different ideas about which crystals to use for the chakras and which crystals to use for healing in general. As you learn more about crystals, you will find that there are also a lot of different and occasionally conflicting statements about them. I have found the following sources to contain the most reliable crystal information as a general rule:

- *The Crystal Bible, Crystal Users Guide, The Encyclopedia of Crystals*, or *The Illustrated Guide to Crystals* by Judy Hall
- *The Book of Stones* by Robert Simmons and Naisha Ahsian
- *Love Is In The Earth* by Melody

Making a Personal Medicine Bag

Making a medicine bag you can wear is one way to use crystals for protection and spirit connection. Exactly what you want in the bag depends on your personal needs and preferences. The contents will represent your personal medicine, and each medicine bag is unique.

Ideally you would make the bag of natural fabric. Silk or cotton would work, but I have found that leather is generally best for durability. You can use elk, buffalo, or deer hide, with cow hide being the last resort. Often I have seen a bag then put into the shell of a turtle.

North America is called Turtle Island by some indigenous people. An old native legend tells of the turtle offering to hold the soil from the bottom of the ocean on his back and how that soil multiplied, creating the land on which we now live. We honor the turtle by using his cast-off shell. However, remember that it is never acceptable to kill an animal just to use a part of its anatomy.

All medicine bags should start with the seven chakras crystals. Star energy connects to these crystals, and when they are all together, they create the whole communication circuit, which is rather like a radio circuit.

1. When making the bag, pray over each crystal, being mindful of your intention of what you need each stone to do as you put them in the bag one by one. Focusing on each stone will help, and you will have an understanding what each crystal represents. (You may want to refer to the chakra information in chapter 9.) A good medicine bag might include the following selection:
   - Amethyst to keep your crown chakra open and keep you connected to spirit.
   - Herkimer Diamond to aid your ability to interpret spiritual information.
   - Lapis to help you share the information you have received.
   - Rose Quartz to receive and express unconditional love.

- Green Flourite to help you integrate the spiritual and earth energies and to balance emotions.
- Black Tourmaline to be creative, focused, and inspirational.
- Smoky Quartz to plant your roots into the Earth and to become grounded, stable, and secure.

2. After praying over each crystal, smudge it with white sage (pass it through the smoke of white sage burning in a container with sage embers).
3. Place some white sage in the bag with the stones. (The sage should not be burning or smoldering.)
4. You may also add some tobacco, which is considered a sacred plant by Native Americans.
5. As you walk through life, you can add to your medicine bag. Add additional items that are meaningful to you such as a small replica of your totem animal or its picture. Honor your totem animal(s) with its inclusion. Another item might be something representative of your goals in life. Some individuals also include pieces of red, white, yellow, and black cotton to represent the four compass directions.

Handle your medicine bag with respect and love. Put it by your medicine wheel or on your altar when you are not carrying it with you. Don't just throw it around. Wearing it is a way of honoring and letting it help you. If you do not wear it, you are not honoring it.

Protection for Your Home

If many people move in and out of your home, you would benefit from placing something above your doorway for protection. The traditional way was to put tobacco ties above the door; however, crystals can also be used. Place the appropriate crystals in a cotton cloth or leather pouch. Periodically cleanse them by smudging them with white sage because they absorb negative energy.

It's important to have an open home where visitors feel welcome. But you have to understand that many visitors may bring their difficulties and stresses with them. People need the comfort of friendship, but they can inadvertently bring negative energies with them. If you place the appropriate crystals above your doorway, those stones will help balance the energy entering your home.

Which crystals you use will depend upon your home's needs. A good way to start is by using a crystal for each of the four compass directions—yellow for the east, red for the south, black for the west, and white for the north.

Here is a sample mix of stones representing the different elements to put in your home protection bag to help the home stay clear of negative energy.

- Kyenite to absorb negativity. This is a good stone that never needs to be cleansed.
- Black stones such as tourmaline, obsidian, or black onyx can also absorb and disperse negative energy. I keep an obsidian obelisk in my home and counseling office.
- A clear quartz for purity of thoughts, as well as the sky and Spirit, is recommended.
- A rose quartz is symbolic of the heart, and as you know, your home is where your heart is.
- A smoky quartz represents the fact that you have a home built upon the earth but are connected to spirit.
- An amethyst is also suggested to represent Spirit.
- Malachite suggests abundance.

A Wake-Up Call!

Crystals not only represent the energy of the earth but also Spirit, as they hold the sacred flame within them. They also make wonderful gifts. Use them abundantly.

CHAPTER 18

The Medicine Wheel of Life

(The true Indian) sees no need for setting apart one day in seven as a holy day, because to him all days are God's days. The American mingled with his pride a singular humility. Spiritual arrogance was foreign to his nature and teaching.

—Ohiyesa of the Santee Sioux
(Charles Alexander Eastman)

What the Medicine Wheel Represents

The medicine wheel is an ancient symbol. Some version of it is used by almost all native peoples in the Americas and across the world. The symbol of the medicine wheel can be found on many Native American artifacts, and much has been written about it. It represents the Circle of Life and the cycle of all things that exist in the ever-moving Universe.

The information for this chapter comes from my spirit guidance and also my personal study of and work with various medicine wheels in the Southwest.

Let's take a look at the term *medicine wheel* and analyze what the name signifies for many indigenous peoples.

I have been told by varied tribal members that the term *medicine* means knowledge. Knowledge then results in wisdom, and wisdom ultimately brings power. So *medicine* can be defined as "power of wisdom."

Wheel on the other hand, represents the endless circle. Indigenous people consider the circle a sacred symbol because the circle has no beginning or end, no up or down; everything is equal and in balance. The circle connects everything. Observation shows that many things in the natural world are in a circle; the sun, the moon, the planets, and the seasons all travel in a circle.

A direct definition of what the medicine wheel represents would be, "a sacred circle of wisdom and power." The medicine wheel represents birth, death, and rebirth; the cycles of the seasons; the movement of energy; and our journeys through life—all parts of endless circles. The medicine wheel is a tool to help humankind understand the big picture, those ideas and concepts that are not visible or tangible. It helps us look at our lives as we move around the spokes of the wheel to evaluate our progress and to correct those areas in need.

The Big Horn medicine wheel in Wyoming has twenty-eight individual spokes. Those spokes are thought to represent the lunar calendar. I believe they were used as a reminder of daily tasks for tribal members to complete during each cycle. This was part of the indigenous lifestyle and worship.

Indigenous peoples believed that there was an energetic medicine wheel in the sky and a corresponding one in the center of the earth.

This is another part of the basis for the concept of *as above, so below*. The meaning of *as above, so below* is that whatever happens on Earth is also happening in the sky. As the people worshiped and honored life tasks, they were bringing down star energy to generate balance and harmony in life.

The medicine wheel consists of a cross within a circle. The cross symbolizes the Native American four compass directions, but also the ancient Celtic cross with its four equal arms. The circle represents the Sacred Hoop spoken of by Back Elk and others. (See illustration 3.)

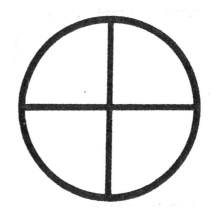

- The vertical arms of the cross symbolize our spiritual connection to the sky and the earth. This is the realm of Spirit, connecting to the physical realm of the earth.
- The horizontal arms of the cross signify our interconnection to each other and everything around us.

The human body also fits within the circle of the medicine wheel. The cross within the wheel illustrates how the human body is like the Tree of Life. The vertical arms of the cross represent the body from head to feet. The head, like the branches of a tree, reaches to the sky while the feet, like roots of a tree, connect into the earth. The horizontal arms of the cross are like human arms stretched out to either side; they encompass and connect to other people, the plants, the animals, and the guides who are with you throughout life. Everything that has to do with the human condition, our personal development, growth, relationships, and lives are within the medicine wheel.

Compass Directions and Colors of Mankind

The medicine wheel has four compass points. These points show how the compass directions—north, south, east, and west—are represented by the colors of mankind's races. However, there are diverse beliefs among the Native American tribes regarding which direction is marked by which color. Regardless of what colors are used, the general concept of what each represents remains the same. These are the color combinations Spirit has advised me to use:

- North represents the white race.
- South represents the red-skinned people.
- East represents the yellow race.
- West represents the black race.

The Elements and Components of Human Nature

The four compass directions of the medicine wheel also hold the gifts from the elements of the physical world—fire, air, water, and earth. Without these elements, life on Earth could not exist. The elements blend easily as they connect with the four components of human nature—mind, body, emotions, and spirit.

- North carries the energy of fire and represents the human spirit.
- South carries the energy of Earth and represents our physical bodies.

- East carries the energy of air and represents the mind with its plans and ideas.
- West carries the energy of water and represents the emotional aspects of our beings.

The very arrangement of where these features are located on the medicine wheel shows an inherent balance. The arrangement also clarifies how humanity fits into the big picture of interconnectedness.

Lessons of the Seasons and Stages of Life

Life, like the four seasons of the year, carries lessons that need to be learned and evaluated. Consider where you would fit into the medicine wheel of life as you evaluate your progress though the years and life stages. The stages of life are youth, adulthood, maturity, and old age. The lessons are as follows:

- On the east arm of the medicine wheel cross are the lessons of spring and youth: new beginnings, planting new seeds, generating new ideas or projects, creativity, rebirth/renewal and education to enhance the mind.
- On the south arm are summer and adulthood: the need for growth and nurturing of the seeds you planted in the spring. It's time to develop relationships and careers but also to balance play and work and learn responsibility to the earth and caring for your body.
- On the west arm are the lessons of fall and maturity/late adulthood. It's time to harvest what you have nurtured in the summer. There is need for emotional analysis and introspection as you approach second chances to fulfill your dreams.

- On the north arm are the lessons of winter and old age; these are endings, the need for healing, connecting to Spirit, and gratitude for what you have received. There is a need to share with others what you have and your life wisdom as an Elder.

To achieve a healthy balanced life, equal development in all areas of life stages is important. Awareness of the need to work on each area and the will to do so will aid in your development of higher awareness. (See illustration 4.)

North
White Race
Fire Element
Spirit
Winter
Old Age
Gratitude and Sharing

West
Black Race
Water Element
Emotions
Fall
Late Adulthood
Introspection and Harvest

East
Yellow Race
Air Element
Mind
Spring
Youth
New Beginnings

South
Red Race
Earth Element
Physical Body
Summer
Early Adulthood
Development of Relationships/Career

Building the Medicine Wheel

Having a medicine wheel in your home is a useful reminder of what needs to be done and also to attract and to balance life energy. There are many ways to build a medicine wheel, indoors or out. But at this time a small crystal one located in your personal spiritual sanctuary would be a good idea. The energy of the crystals can help you connect to the stars and help your heart release unconditional love. Later you may wish to build a medicine wheel outdoors large enough to hold several persons for meditation, ceremony, or prayer. My personal wheel is about eight inches in diameter, and the stone sizes are about one inch, with a clear quartz point measuring three inches high in the center.

For a simple and basic medicine wheel you will need these supplies:

A. Leather or cotton cloth a little larger than the size of the medicine wheel you plan to make.

B. A clear quartz polished point crystal about three inches in height.

C. Four pieces of tumbled amethyst a little larger than one inch in size.

D. Sixteen or more tumbled one-inch pieces of clear quartz (four for each section).

E. Sixteen or more tumbled one-inch pieces of rose quartz (four for each section).

F. Four obsidian pieces about one inch in size.

Building a medicine wheel is sacred work and should be done with reverence and a positive intention of connecting to a higher power. Show respect for the Spirit with love and gratitude for your blessings. Pray as you place the stones. Don't forget to smudge the location and all the components, as well as yourself, before you start building the medicine wheel. After your wheel is built, send it love and gratitude as you use it to for your spiritual practices. Always thank the medicine wheel and All That Is for their help.

Medicine Wheel Setup

See illustration 5 for a sample of a fully set up medicine wheel. The instructions are as follows:

1. Create a sacred space by setting the array of gemstones on a surface such as a piece of leather, cotton cloth, or other natural product that stands between it and whatever solid surface the medicine wheel is placed upon.

2. The center stone represents the Oneness/the Creator and is a polished clear quartz point crystal. Clear quartz is considered the master stone and a base from which several other stones develop under heat and pressure over time. This should be the biggest stone in the array.

3. Place an amethyst representing the spiritual connection to the Creator in each of the four compass directions. The amethysts should be about three or four inches away from the center point. These should be the second largest stones. Start in the east, the new beginnings. Then proceed in a clockwise direction to the south, the west, and finally the north.

4. Between the amethyst compass points, going in a clockwise direction around the perimeter of the medicine wheel, place at least four pieces of small clear quartz. It is beneficial if they touch, but this is not required. These clear quartz crystals seal the connection among all the energies of the medicine wheel.

5. Inside the medicine wheel, between the center stone and each of the four compass points where the amethyst stands, place several rose quartz pieces. The rose quartz represents unconditional love for you and all that exists in the Universe. This stone also signifies the will to be of service to others without expecting anything in return.

6. Place an obsidian piece in the east direction, just inside the perimeter of the wheel and directly behind the amethyst. Next, place an obsidian piece behind the amethyst in the south, west, and north directions. The obsidian brings a grounding energy that represents the connection between the earth and the Universe.

If you choose to incorporate the colors of the directions, place the amethyst and obsidian on a yellow circle for the east, a black circle in the west, a red circle in the south, and a white circle in the north. You may also place the center stone on a purple circle if you so desire. The color circles should be made of natural fabric or leather.

If crystals are not available, improvise with something that is representative of the same energy. Remember that everything contains life energy and has an energy vibration. I have seen medicine wheels built with pine cones, rocks, and a variety of natural objects because that was all that was available. A very simple and basic wheel can be built in nature with just the center stone and the four compass stores represented. When working with the medicine wheel in prayer or ceremony, always smudge yourself first and then enter and leave by the east door, as this is the pathway of new beginnings. Be grateful for what you have, your gifts from the Creator.

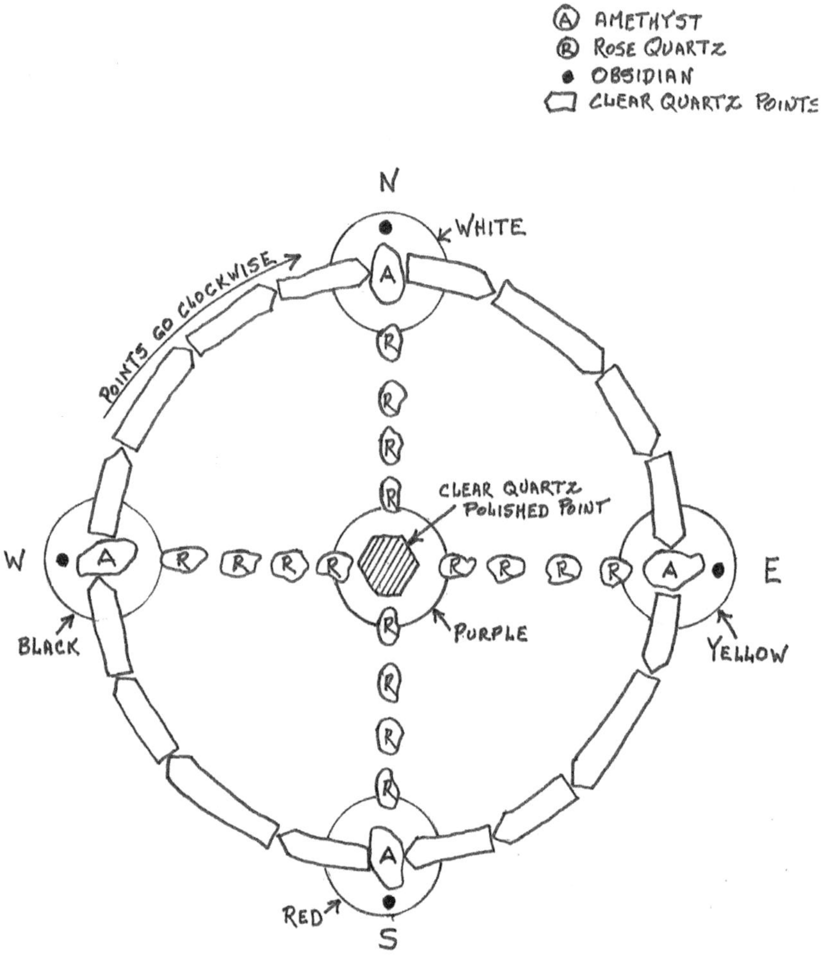
A AMETHYST
R ROSE QUARTZ
OBSIDIAN
CLEAR QUARTZ POINTS
N
WHITE
POINTS GO CLOCKWISE
CLEAR QUARTZ POLISHED POINT
W
E
BLACK
PURPLE
YELLOW
RED
S

Creating a Living Community Medicine Wheel

It is easy to do a simple ceremony, hold a prayer gathering with several individuals whose focus is to make a spiritual connection, send healing energy to the earth, or perform other similar tasks. Place a symbolic item such as a clear quartz or amethyst in the center of the circle to represent the Creator energy. Acknowledge the four compass directions and stand in a circle holding hands while sending love, gratitude, and prayers to the Creator.

This simple exercise can be used to create a ceremony designed to attract light energy needed to cleanse and support Mother Earth. Honor the four compass directions and hold the vision of a new earth with clean water, fresh air, fertile soil, no wars or conflicts, and compassionate humans living in balance and harmony with All That Is.

A Wake-Up Call!

Spirit's message is,

> *When people gather together in a circle, the spiritual flame in their hearts grows large. The flame is everyone's joint energy; this same flame is also within the center of the earth.*

This reason is why humanity needs to do more ceremonies, to bring down the star energy, to nurture the flame in the center of the planet Earth.

CHAPTER 19

Balancing Emotions—Bach®
Flower Remedies to the Rescue

Till now, man has been up against Nature; from now on,
he will be up against his own nature.
—Dennis Gabor, *Inventing the Future*, 1963

As humans we are spirit, mind, body, and emotions. Everything you think and do affects your energy field and the energy field of those around you. Every symptom you have can be related back to one or more of your chakra energy centers. If you are feeling down because you've had a bad day, acknowledge it and then let it go. Silently holding onto negative feelings and emotions damages the body. Emotions such as anger, sorrow, resentment, and guilt act like hidden intruders, robbing you of the joy and the peace of mind you deserve.

Verbal disagreements can be discussed and dissipated. But nonverbal disagreements, with their attached negative emotions, also need to be cleared from your energy field. If you hold on to those emotions, they will act like a caustic acid to weaken your energy field and leave you vulnerable to illness. The very name, *disease*, provides us with an indication of what it takes for illness to begin.

Louise Hay, in her classic books *You Can Heal Your Life* and *Heal Your Body*, explains how mental patterns can create disease in the body.

Carolyn Myss, in *Anatomy of the Spirit*, talks about fifteen years of research on energy medicine and claims that every illness corresponds to a pattern of emotional and psychological stresses, beliefs, and attitudes. Illness can be healed by connecting to an inner and outer spirituality.

Deepak Chopra says that every cell in your body is always listening to your thoughts and emotions.

Dr. Edward Bach, a well-known and respected English physician, bacteriologist, immunologist, and homeopath, in the 1930s, was very much in agreement. As a result, he was not satisfied with the fact that traditional medicine treated like symptoms and illnesses with the same type of medication. Dr. Bach felt that a physician must consider the individual's personality, emotions, and lifestyle when treating a patient.

Psychoneuroimmunology investigates how the mind and body work together to create or heal illness. Scientific research has shown that there is an interaction that exists between the psychological processes and the nervous and immune systems of the human body. Current research proves that Dr. Bach was on the right track and ahead of his medical contemporaries.

Dr. Bach also approached physical health from a spiritual perspective. He stated in *Heal Thyself* that "disease is entirely the result of a conflict between our spiritual and mortal selves." He went on to explain that our souls are immortal and know what our purposes in life are. We are born in life situations to best learn the lessons necessary to accomplish our life purposes. However, our personalities and lives themselves can create interference that conflicts with our original intents. As a result of that conflict, we lose our emotional balance and allow emotions like fear, doubt, anger, worry, and disappointment to enter our lives. These and other emotions are the "root cause" of disease.

As a result of his connection to nature from an early age, that is where Dr. Bach looked for answers in trying to develop a safe and simple self-help system of healing. Dr. Bach felt that he was "divinely guided" to find the healing modalities that God had placed in nature for the prevention and cure of disease.

I have heard an old indigenous legend about why illness exists and healing that can be found in nature. A condensed version of the legend is as follows:

Once, a very long time ago, people, animals, and plants could talk to each other. For a long time things went smoothly and everyone lived in harmony with each other. No one took more than they needed for nourishment from the plants or killed more animals than they could eat. They always consumed everything they took. Then two human brothers got bored with life and decided to start a contest with each other to see who was the better hunter. They killed indiscriminately and left dead animals to rot. Soon others joined the contest.

The animals became concerned that if this human behavior continued, soon they would become extinct. The animals called for a council to decide what to do. All animals sent representatives, and they spoke long and hard with many ideas being presented. Finally they settled on the idea that for every transgression of the Universal Laws there would be a consequence. The consequences varied depending on the seriousness of the transgression and included different illnesses.

When the plants heard about the animal council's decision, they thought it was too severe. Their point of view was that humans didn't mean to do serious harm, they were just uninformed. So the plants came up with their own decision. For every illness that the animals handed out, the plants would carry a cure for it within their own kingdom.

It is interesting to note that much of our medicine is based on plant elements.

Dr. Bach, spent years researching, testing the remedies on himself, and working with patients before he found the thirty-eight flower essences that are part of today's system. The flower essences are also known as flower remedies.

He divided the Bach® Flower Remedies into seven groups representing specific emotional categories of basic conflicts that create interference. Each group then addresses the multifaceted emotions that fit within that grouping.

The following is an overview of the negative emotional states each Fflower Eessence attacks to help us regain balance and aid the body in healing. The essences are not designed to replace medical attention but rather to serve as supplemental tools for emotional balance and enhanced well-being. The essences work equally well for human, plants, and animals.

Fear

Aspen—anxiety from an unknown source during the day or night. Useful for nightmares.

Cherry Plum—fear of losing control and doing something impulsive or harmful (e.g., road rage).

Mimulus—fear of specific known things, such as dogs, financial problems, the dark, or death.

Red Chestnut—excessive fear and worry about other people's welfare. Useful for caregivers.

Rock Rose—abject, frozen in fear, and terror.

Uncertainty

Cerato—indecisiveness from lack of trusting own judgment, a tendency to always ask for advice.

Gentian—discouragement and doubt after suffering some sort of setback.

Gorse—depression, hopelessness, and despair.

Hornbeam—mental weariness, procrastination because of overwork or lack of enthusiasm for it.

Scleranthus—indecisiveness from lack of being able to choose. Does not ask for advice.

Wild Oat—uncertain as to what path to take in life.

Insufficient Interest in Present Circumstances

Chestnut Bud—failure to learn from past mistakes when making new decisions.

Clematis—daydreamers living in their own worlds, absent minded, not focused on present.

Honeysuckle—focused on past memories rather than present circumstances. Nostalgic.

Mustard—depression that descends for no apparent reason. Can't shake it off.

Olive—mental and physical exhaustion after a long period of stress or overwork.

White Chestnut—inability to shut down a mind filled with nonstop thoughts or worry.

Wild Rose—resignation, apathy and lack of enthusiasm for changing unpleasant life situations.

Loneliness

Heather—self-centered and talkative about personal issues. No interest in others' problems.

Impatiens—easily irritated by the slowness of others. Impatient, independent, accident prone.

Water Violet—very private and aloof. Tends to withdraw rather than socialize.

Oversensitivity to Influences and Ideas

Agrimony—hiding internal conflicts and problems from self and others behind a happy face. Often may use alcohol, other drugs, or food as a pain reliever.

Centaury—can't say no. Passive and anxious to please with a tendency to become subservient.

Holly—envy, jealousy, hatred, and general anger toward others. Can't open heart to love.

Walnut—helps adapt to change and disconnect from what is no longer needed. Protects from unwanted outside influences.

Despondency and Despair

Crab Apple—cleansing energy to feel better about one's unpleasant appearance or experiences.

Elm—for feelings of being overwhelmed because of workload or responsibility. Overload may also lead to a loss of self-confidence.

Larch—lack of self-confidence.

Oak—driven by duty to keep trying, even in the face of exhaustion which may lead to depression.

Pine—guilt and shame from blaming self for everyone's mistakes. A sense of unworthiness.

Star of Bethlehem—aftereffects from any form of trauma or shock, loss, or grief.

Sweet Chestnut—mental and emotional anguish, at the limit of endurance but not suicidal.

Willow—neutralizes feelings of resentment and self-pity.

Overcare for the Welfare of Others

Beech—for those who love to criticize others and feel they are always right. Intolerance.

Chicory—possessive and self-serving love. Can't give without getting something back.

Rock Water—impose high standards on self to the point of martyrdom. Lack of flexibility.

Vervain—enthusiastic about a cause and tries to convince others. Finds relaxing difficult.

Vine—dictatorial and inflexible behavior. My way or the highway thinking.

Rescue Remedy

Dr. Bach combined five of the thirty-eight essences to create Rescue Remedy, which is considered to be a leading stress-relief formula. He combined Star of Bethlehem, Impatiens, Rock Rose, Clematis, and Cherry Plum, to bring about about a sense of calm and a feeling of control almost immediately upon use. Rescue Remedy and its companion Rescue Remedy Cream are well-known and used in sixty-six countries around the world.

In the United States, the products can be found in most health food grocery stores, many pet stores, and therapy offices. Medical doctors, psychiatrists, chiropractors, and veterinarians recommend and use them. The Bach Flower Essences are completely safe and natural. They can be used in combination with any other medications or foods that a person is consuming, without fear of any adverse reactions.

Choosing the proper Bach® Flower Essence to match your mood is aided by the self-help tools generally available at the point of purchase. To use the essences, put two drops in a glass of water, coffee, soda, or other beverage and sip at intervals, repeating as often as necessary. Rescue Remedy requires four drops because it is a blend of essences.

Animals respond to the flower essences equally well and are extensively used by pet owners. Mimulus is an excellent remedy for animals who fear thunderstorms or the noise associated with the Fourth of July. The administration dosage is primarily the same as for humans. Two drops from a 10-milliliter stock bottle can be put in the drinking water of eight ounces or less, on the food, or on the animal's paws, nose, or ears where the hair is more sparse. For Rescue Remedy, the dosage is four drops. For large animals like horses, adjust the dosage upwards.

Plants thrive under the care of the flower essences. Rescue Remedy in the water will help cut flowers last longer. It also helps plants that are injured, neglected, or transplanted.

For additional information contact a Bach Foundation Registered Practitioner from the international list at www.bachcentre.com. Alternate information resources is available on my website, www.ancientspiritwisdom.com, or at www.bachremedies.com or www.bachflowereducation.com.

A Wake-Up Call!

Dr. Gerber, in his book *Vibrational Medicine*, called The Bach Flower Essences the medicine of the future. As a therapist, I have found the Bach® Flower Essences to be an extremely useful tool in helping clients cope with the challenges and emotions of life.

CHAPTER 20

Light Exercises

An angel can illuminate the thoughts and mind of man by strengthening the power of vision.

—St. Thomas Aquinas

The Council tells me,

Spiritual law says it is important to take care of the Spirit first and the body second because everything begins with Spirit. Recognize that spiritual energy has created everything that exists, and if your internal focus is on a higher power [your version of God], then it does not matter how that focus is expressed externally. Your heart, your meditation, and your intention will demonstrate that higher power focus in how you live. If you honor the spirit within your body first, that action gets translated to mean, "I'm going to honor Spirit by taking care of my body."

As long as you stay aligned with the Spirit and follow your heart, everything will get taken care of in the spiritual world. However, in the linear physical world where you live, everything will not be taken care of unless you actively work on bringing light energy into your body. The process of bringing in light energy is like water turning into ice, metaphorically speaking. The original energy of light is the same. It's just changed to a new form.

Taking care of your body is also considered doing light work. Since breath itself is light energy, bringing more light into your body through breath work is an important practice of self-care. As you breathe in connect with and focus on each breath of air and more light will enter your body.

This basic centering exercise is designed to balance and energize your personal energy field. However, while doing the exercise, it is important to hold the intent of bringing in the light and grounding yourself to the earth. Rubber soles can create interference, so take your shoes off and have your feet flat on the floor.

Basic Centering Technique

If you choose, you can smudge yourself prior to doing the exercise to cleanse your energy. Do the centering technique slowly and consciously, taking the time to feel the energy flow. The basic technique for centering is as follows:

- Visualize a bright star above your head. See bright white light coming from it and pouring into your crown chakra like water pouring out of a pitcher.

- See the light coming into the top of your head. Feel the warmth and love as the energy flows down your body, passing through each of your chakras.
- Visualize the light spreading into every cell of your being until your whole body feels like it's vibrating with the energy.
- Feel the energy moving down your arms to your hands and down your legs to your feet.
- Visualize the energy flowing out the soles of your feet and into the ground, as though you were growing roots that connect you to Mother Earth.

You should now feel centered and grounded. If not, repeat the exercise using your imagination until you do. This exercise is also useful to do before meditation and when you are feeling scattered or overwhelmed. Once you have done it a few times, you can do it very quickly at any time or place necessary.

Meditative Breath Exercise

Each person has his or her own rhythm of breathing, so use a speed that is comfortable to you. The important thing is to feel the depth of each breath as you inhale. Put your hand on your solar plexus, just below your heart, so you can feel how deep you are breathing. Make each breath fill your lungs to the very bottom.

1. Take three deep, slow breaths in a row. As you inhale through your nose, visualize the light entering your body through the top your head. As you exhale, blow the air out though your mouth. Feel the light coming in and going out every cell of your body.

2. Visualize the bright star above your head. Feel the warmth of the light energy. The heat coming from the star as if you were sitting under the hot midday sun.

3. Take another three deep breaths. Feel the light coming into your crown chakras.

4. By the time you take the third breath, the light has gone all the way through your energy centers, down through your hands and feet, out your fingers and the soles of your feet.

5. See the light coming out your fingertips, your toes, and every pore of your skin. Visualize a light shield forming all around your body. Let it circle around you in a clockwise fashion, above and below you.

6. Continue to breathe deeply at your own speed and rhythm. Feel yourself connected to the earth and the sky as you feel the heat of the energy making you warmer and warmer.

7. Now you are in the center of a light sphere. Feel the warmth that is emanating from you.

8. Position your hands palms upward, continue to breathe in the light energy of Spirit for as long as you would like.

9. Say thank you at the end of each meditation or breathing exercise because you are acknowledging the gift of life.

This exercise is good to do on a daily basis, even if it is as short as five minutes. Use it to raise your level of awareness and to strengthen your energy body, your aura. It also helps to bring in more light for the world, and you are the channel through which the light comes. Receive with humility and love, and in humility and love give back to others who are in need. That action is known as walking the spiritual road and being of service to others.

Releasing Techniques

If things are not going well in your life and you need to get rid of unwanted attitudes, behaviors, and beliefs, the following exercises can be useful. These exercises must be done in a serious manner and with a heart full of love and gratitude, or they will not be effective. Spirit gives based on your ability to have faith and to receive. Exercise A can be used for personal work or to help others. Exercise B is to be used for personal work only.

Exercise A

1. Center and clear yourself by performing the grounding exercise at the beginning of this chapter.
2. Mentally dig a large hole and put all the problems of the people you are trying to help into the hole and cover them.
3. Pray for assistance and ask for whatever it is that you need to achieve your goals.
4. Thank the Universe and your guides for helping you.

Exercise B

You will need two small stones for this exercise. One should be a black crystal (e.g., tourmaline, jet, or obsidian). If a crystal is not available, substitute a black river rock or something similar. The other stone should be a clear quartz or a Herkimer diamond. An alternative stone would be any kind of white rock.

1. Find a private, quiet spot in nature, a nonrocky spot by a moving stream or a body of water, if possible. Do not use a still water.

2. Center and clear yourself by performing the grounding exercise.

3. Hold the black stone in your hand of preference for sending energy. (I'm right-handed, so it's in my right hand.) The Herkimer diamond/white stone is in your other hand to receive energy.

4. Pray and ask the universal powers to help you put the negativity or whatever issue you are working to eliminate into the black stone. Focus on the matter and will the issue to come out of your life and go into the black stone.

5. Ask for the void that is left as a result of the clearing to be filled with light, love, and gratitude. Focus on the Herkimer diamond and let the light energy flow from the Universe through the stone and into you.

6. Thank the Universe and your spirit guide(s) for their assistance.

7. Toss the black stone into the running water or stream so it can be cleansed and have its energy transmuted. If running water is not available, dig a hole in the earth and bury the black stone deeply enough that it will not be disturbed. Then ask the earth to cleanse it.

8. Place the Herkimer diamond/white stone in your medicine pouch or on your medicine wheel, your altar, or in another sacred place.

Hopefully these exercises will help you create what you would like to see in the world. If all people do their part to raise their consciousness to bring light and love into the world and to our planet, the future will be as bright as predicted by the Mayans in the coming Shift. Send light and love to All That Is.

A Wake-Up Call!

Most of us are familiar with the children's story of the three little pigs. The pigs were trying to avoid being lunch for the wolf, so they each built a house to protect themselves. For building materials, one used straw, another built with sticks, and the third one used brick to keep the wolf out. Only the brick house withstood the wolf's efforts to blow it down. It seems that often humanity's approach to life is similar to the philosophy of the three little pigs.

Some individuals think this life is all there is; they do not believe in any higher power. They think that it is important to play and enjoy life to the fullest without thinking about any consequences of their choices. Sometimes they hide their fears and doubts in violent or risky behaviors or in alcohol and other drugs. They escape reality in whatever way they can. Life is now, and then it's all over. This house seems to be built of straw.

Another group is only interested in acquiring all the power, money, control, "toys" (whatever they may represent) that they can. They believe in the notion that he who dies with the most "toys" wins. We should see this as a sad and self-centered way to live. This is building with sticks.

The third group is the ones who are looking for and making spiritual connections and raising their consciousness levels; they are the light workers and seekers of the truth who build with bricks.

Which group are you in?

CHAPTER 21

How Spirit Has Guided My Life

I conceive that the land belongs to a vast family of which many are dead, few are living, and countless members are still to be born.

—A chieftain from Nigeria

My life-path of spiritual growth has been convoluted, incorporating many life lessons along the way. In my wildest dreams, I could never have imagined the drastic shifts I've lived through. I've gone from a homeless refugee to a talk show host, psychotherapist, and now an author. I've had several near death experiences, but I'm happy and healthy. The following is a slice of my history to give you an insight into my world.

I was born in Liepaja, Latvia (one of the Baltic states bordering Russia), to a well-to-do family with strong ties to the land on our large farm. My memories go back to the age of eighteen months. During my early, impressionable years, I learned about connecting with nature, spirits, and the human soul from my mother, Alma, who was part of a long line of Latvian artists and musicians. My mother would also share wisdom about the healing properties of plants on our regular nature walks. My favorite times were spent in the garden or the woods, under a tree. As an only child, my favorite companion was the weeping birch by the kitchen door. I dreamed of being a writer while playing and helping my mother care for the ducks, chickens, rabbits, and other small farm animals.

However, the hissing gander that chased and bit me was one lesson I would just as soon have skipped. Another time, the sight of the bloody destruction done to the rabbit hutches by a fox during the night taught me about death. Today that information and those experiences serve not only as a precious connection to my childhood but also as a firm base for my work with clients.

When I was about five years old, life shifted. My family had to, literally, walk away from all our holdings with the advance of Stalin's Russian army in World War II. As aristocratic land owners, we were in danger. If captured, my parents would have been killed or sent to icy Siberia for slave labor, and I would have been sent to a communist school for youth. The focus of the youth school was to reprogram and indoctrinate the children to become part of the communist youth movement. (Incidentally this is the same type of technique used by the varied governments, including the United States in the 1800s when mandating boarding schools for Native American children as part of disrupting the indigenous cultures.)

As World War II raged across Europe, my family and I often barely escaped with our lives. We walked away from our beloved home with only what we could wear or carry. That load also included food to last the family several days. I had my own little suitcase, which I could barely carry but was responsible for anyway because that's how it had to be. There was no other choice. Responsibility came at an early age. Those were difficult times, but it was going to get worse.

Just before we reached land borders out of Latvia, they were closed by the Russians. Escape by land was no longer possible. Everyone fleeing to safety had but one choice, turn toward the sea. This meant another long walk for our weary family.

Many, many days later we finally arrived at the Baltic Sea shore. We were fortunate. The German navy was preparing to retreat and were willing to take as many refugees on the ships, as they could carry. Those brave and caring German sailors risked their own lives saving the refugees. As we sailed out of the harbor in the city of Liepaja, the German battleships were so loaded that they would have started to take on water if one more person were to come aboard. To see the throngs of refugees still left behind on the shore was heartbreaking. The Russian guns were blazing, and shells sailed over the crowded decks as the ships pulled out to sea. It's a miracle that these ships, heavily laden with their human cargo, did not sink. One kind German sailor even shared his fish sandwich with me when he realized I was starving.

All the Latvian refugees were dropped off on German soil, and the ships continued on with their war efforts. All of us refugees were now totally on our own. My family and I walked across Germany, catching rides and doing day labor where and when we could find it. Food and shelter were scarce. The German people were kind and helpful, often creating work so they could feed or shelter us for a short time. Once after not having eaten for several days, we were so hungry that we ate grass.

During this time there were many air raids. Surviving bombs and bullets were daily events. It was necessary to sneak through the woods in the daytime because American war planes would strafe the streets with bullets if they saw any people. War seems to bring out the worst in humans on both sides of a conflict.

After the end of World War II, our family became part of the flood of displaced persons (DPs) going to varied countries. In 1949, my family was sponsored by a Mississippi business owner willing to help DPs in exchange for labor. Upon arrival in the United States, we were housed in a small one-room cabin with no running water. I believe these were old slave cabins. We spent one year on that Mississippi farm, working off the expenses of the immigration sponsorship.

The cultural differences made for a frightening and difficult time for the whole family, especially my parents. However, the snakes (including cotton mouths), crickets, wasps, and praying mantises were a whole new world for me to explore. Again, my connection to nature was an important link that helped me through the transition. I believe Spirit was teaching life lessons about coping with fear, loss, grief, change, survival, and self-sufficiency to strengthen and prepare me for helping others later.

At school they taught me English by pointing to objects or pictures and saying the corresponding word. I remember one time when another student grabbed me by the hand and pulled me outside to teach me the word "ant." Everyone made teaching me a class project because I was such a novelty.

It didn't take long for a nine-year-old to catch on. Soon I was skipping grades because my European education was more advanced than that of my third-grade classmates. (My mother had taught me how to read, write in script, add, subtract, divide, and multiply through six before I started school.)

American history however, was another matter. I had no knowledge that there was a group of people known as Native Americans in this new land. I did not know anything about American history and had never seen a movie, let alone a cowboy and Indian movie. I hadn't even read any books about it. These topics were not discussed at school. So it was a total surprise one night when I was eleven years old when I started a dream that was to last for seven nights. Each night it picked up the story from where it had left off the previous night. (The indigenous cultures call these type of dreams "medicine dreams." These dreams serve to connect us to a higher level of wisdom and information.)

This dream was in full color and featured a five-year-old white girl living in a small Midwest community during the settlement of the old West. Her parents were both killed during an Indian raid. But as often was the case, the Lakota raiding party took her with them as they left. The Chief of the Lakota tribe adopted her and raised her as his own daughter. The dream progressed to give extensive information, to explain the spirituality and indigenous way of life. The girl learned the Lakota culture and became one of the tribe spiritually, mentally, emotionally, and physically. She married a young brave. Life was good. She was very happy.

However, the people in the white settlement had never forgotten that she had been kidnapped from the raid where her parents died. After a period of time, the Anglos discovered where she was and went to get her. From their perspective, they were "rescuing" her by bringing her back to "civilization." The now grown young woman was very sad and felt lost in the white world, which she had forgotten. Repeatedly she tried to escape back to what she felt was her real home, but she was never successful. This is where the dream stopped on the seventh day.

That dream left a very strong impression on me. Decades later it feels like a former life experience. This was the first of many insights that I was to have into my former lives. Many of those lives were spent as a healer and teacher. In my writings, I draw on the information gained through my dreams and past life recall experiences.

As I grew up, I learned to fit into my new life in America, to adjust and explore new goals. But the desire to write a book was never too far from the surface. Then a new urge took over. The need to do spiritual work, perhaps become a missionary or a minister. Out of necessity, I went into the business world but wound up writing and offering assistance to those in need.

When I had the opportunity to move to Arizona, I was thrilled. The desert, with its vast unpopulated spaces and searing sun, terrified me at first. It wasn't long before I discovered that the desert was a spiritual place where much exists under the surface. I developed a love for the desert's secret abundance of life and harsh beauty in spending many hours exploring its secrets.

One day while taking a walk in the desert I encountered a sparkling cavern. Clear quartz crystals sparkled from every angle and stalactites clung to the ceiling. Clusters of the beautifully clear master healing stone clung to the walls and were scattered along the floor. It was like being in a crystal palace with bright light beaming acceptance and love from all directions. It felt very sacred, beautiful, and peaceful. I marked the spot carefully so I could return, but I was never able to find it again. The landmarks were all there, but the crystal grotto was not. (Was this place a dimensional shift or a portal to somewhere else?)

Arizona was the ideal spot to learn more about Native American spiritual beliefs. As I talked to people and read books, I found that I identified with the indigenous perspectives more and more. Even though I had been raised as a Baptist, I could see many connections between the Native American and my Latvian beliefs and traditions. The bond with Native American culture that my childhood dream had begun was growing stronger.

Unaware of other forces working in my life, I moved from Arizona to Wyoming. I was heading toward new connections that had to be made to move my life in the direction preplanned. Several years later while showing a friend around Cheyenne, I met my husband, Kirk. From the moment we met, it was as if we had known each other all our lives. We both recognized this extraordinary connection. Further exploration shows that we are twin flames who have shared many lifetimes together.

When Kirk decided to enjoy an early retirement, we moved to Colorado, where I could earn my Masters degree in social work from the University of Denver. The Colorado Rocky Mountains offered a heartfelt welcome equal to the bond the Arizona desert had forged. This life lesson shows that specific natural locations do not matter; all of nature brings the same connection and help if we spend time with it.

We were happy, but I felt something was missing. There was an ongoing urge to write a book and become more involved with spiritual work. Then one day, a friend invited me to a group meeting focusing on healing the Sacred Hoop of Life from the vision that Black Elk wrote about in his book, *Black Elk Speaks*. The Sacred Hoop is a Native American concept of the interconnecting of everything that exists in the world. I felt chills go up and down my spine as I agreed to go. (Chills up and down your spine is a signal that the kundalini energy is moving, and I'm told it means you are connecting to universal truth.)

Shortly thereafter, I began to recognize my psychic abilities. I paid closer attention to the visions, dreams, and intuitive information I had been receiving all my life from my spirit guides.

Finally, there was clarity about the book I had longed to write. My book was to be based on ancient wisdom and explain how to apply that information in today's modern world and how to live in balance and harmony. I was guided by Spirit through visions, auditory messages, and intuition to recognize that I had contracted to serve as a teacher and messenger. My role in this lifetime was to help bridge the gap between modern life and ancient wisdom with my writings and workshops. I named my new business Legend Lessons.

Kirk and I were also guided by Spirit to work with and sell crystals. Our job is to help people rejuvenate the spiritual flame that lives within everyone's heart but is often overlooked in today's materialistic society. As a result, Firelight Crystals was born. *Firelight* means that there is a spiritual flame of light within each stone. That crystalline flame stimulates an individual's own heart flame to grow and flourish, increasing their consciousness level. The journey to help others reconnect with the energy of light and spirituality had begun.

As I worked on this book, the prophetic "medicine dreams" started coming with more consistency. I continue to receive knowledge through visions and intuition, plus other light workers who also receive guidance from some portion of the Oneness (e.g., the Council of Light or other spirit guides).

My Wake-Up Call!

A lifelong desire to write a book is finally materializing as the timing becomes right. This is the start of other works yet to come. I feel them inside like babies waiting to be born.

Enjoy your life journey and may you walk in beauty.!

GLOSSARY

Akashic Records—celestial records of all actions, thoughts, and feelings that have occurred or will ever occur for each living entity.

chakra centers—invisible, circular energy centers located in the human body and connected to the adrenal glands. These centers respond to light energy vibrations from the spectrum of the rainbow, as well as our emotions and environment.

Codes of Life—Universal Spiritual Laws, a spiritual expansion of the Ten Commandments to include all life, All That Is.

ley lines—geometrically straight line alignments of ancient ceremonial and cultural interest sites from all over the world. These lines are thousands of years old and are purported to contain electrical or magnetic forces. An energy vortex exists where the ley lines intersect.

light consciousness—spiritual awareness and connection to the Oneness.

Light Council/Star Council—part of the Oneness whose role it is to guide humanity in connecting to their soul, to help humanity remember who they are and where they are from and to wake up. These are the keepers of the Akashic Records and the Voice of Spirit.

light worker—one who knows he or she is connected to and are a part of God, his or her soul is light energy. Light workers are here on Earth to be of service to others, to rekindle the flame of love and light within everyone's heart.

medicine wheel—a symbol of the Universe in many indigenous cultures. It is a teacher and guide to help us gain insights into concepts and meanings of things not tangible. The term *medicine* means knowledge. It helps us to understand how the cycles of life, the elements, compass directions, the colors of man, and so much more fit together. It is a tool to be used in ceremony and life evaluation.

Oneness—an interconnected web of high vibration spiritual energies, like an image of God. A part of God but not God. It is where humanity is originally from.

psychoneuroimmunology—the mind and body connection. The study of the interaction between psychological processes and the nervous and immune systems of the human body.

Red Road—Native American concept of the road of spirituality, harmony, and our personal connection with everything in the natural world. Walking this road is similar to living by the Golden Rule of do unto others, as you would have done unto you.

Sacred Circle/Hoop—a Native American concept of the interconnectedness of All That Is.

shadow side—the negative energy, evil and dark.

shape-shifting—defined by Ted Andrews in *The Art of Shapeshifting* as "the ability to effect a change in oneself, in others or in the substance of the environment. This change can be physical or spiritual."

smudging—a way of using sage (or similar herb) to cleanse energy.

spiritual growth—increasing your spiritual awareness and energy vibration.

subtle energy/ vibrational energy—an invisible, radiant energy field that interacts with human physiology responding to intention and focus. It affects both mind and body. It consists of a vibrational life force (movement of molecules in a high energy state) known as *chi* by the Chinese. It is used in doing therapeutic touch, reiki, energy healing, acupuncture, and many others. Affirmations are based on influencing thoughts and consequent physiology

Tree of Life—the chakra system, a human linkage between the earth and the Universe.

walk-ins—a spirit that takes over another's physical body when the original does not want to continue living. These are exceptional events and generally happen only with the agreement of both souls involved.

DISCUSSION QUESTIONS FOR BOOK GROUPS

By IlgaAnn Bunjer

1. ***Ancient Spirit Wisdom* is written from a personal and spirit guidance perspective with many passages directly attributed to spirit messages.**

---Are spirit messages a valid source of information and can they be trusted? Always?

---How can you tell if the message is coming from a light source or from the astral realm talked about in chapter 12?

2. **Death as a final life ending does not exist is a recurring theme in the book.**

---How would it change the world if more people held that belief?

---How would it change varied religions, e.g. Christianity, Judaism, Muslim, etc.?

---Would it change anything in the funeral process/business?

----Do heaven and hell exist?

----Do you agree with the author on what happens after the physical body stops functioning?

3. **In the book, IlgaAnn talks about her past life experiences.**

---Do you believe in reincarnation? Do animals also come back again?

---How do you think a past life has impacted or influenced a present behavior, thought or feeling?

---Why do you think we do not remember past lives or lessons learned? Wouldn't it be helpful to know some of that information?

---Have you experienced any past life recall experiences or do you think your imagination was working overtime?

4. **In her bio, IlgaAnn talks about being "twin flames" with her husband, Kirk.**

---What are "twin flames"? How is it different from "soul mates"?

---Do you think these concepts really exist? How about "soul families"?

5. **Throughout the book we are told about the indigenous concept that "we are all related" and that there is a "Oneness."**

---What does that mean? How can we apply it in our daily lives?

---Does our culture accept that belief? Do any cultures?

---Do you think we are connected to the stars and the star nation? Any particular star?

6.   **While living in Arizona IlgaAnn experienced a crystal grotto in the desert that she could not find again.**
---Do you think it was a dimensional shift like she proposed? Why?

---What could it have been?

7.   **There is a Wake-Up Call at the end of each chapter and IlgaAnn had a dream where the turkey told her to "get up and teach others to wake-up."**
---What meaning does the book imply to being asleep or to "wake-up"? Do you agree?

---What can we do to help people wake-up? What choice do we have to make?

8.   **On the book's cover, what is the symbolism message of the woman coaching the sun to come up?**

9.   **The book discusses life purpose at length.**
---Have you considered your lifetime as being one day in a universal school?

---What lessons do you think you are here to learn for yourself? . . help others learn?

---Are you working on all 3 levels? Which ones are you doing, now. . .as a teen?

---Are you one of the special light workers here to help humanity? Who else might be?

10. Spirit expands the 10 Commandments in chapter 4.
---Does the expansion seem right to you? Does it make them clearer, easier or harder?

---How would it change the church's behavior if they adapted this version?. . . the world's?

11. The book describes the 13 Levels of Consciousness with the lower levels being connected to both the higher (light) and denser dimensions.
---How is that possible?

---Do you think one can talk to the trees, water, earth spirits? Have you met any elementals?

---Does this division/structure make sense and explain anything?

12. Are there any animals that have special meaning for you, that keep coming up?
---Do animals have souls?

---Can animals be spirit guides or do they just bring messages? Your favorites animals?

---Can animals appear as demons? What are demons and where do they come from?

13. **The Medicine Wheel explains our interconnection.**

---Do you think it's valid?

---Where do you see yourself on the Wheel? What message does it bring you?

14. **Can you accept the author's perception of God and Religion or do you disagree?**

ABOUT THE AUTHOR

IlgaAnn Bunjer, MSW, BFRP, is a minister, a psychic, and a therapist who brings together traditional, holistic, and shamanic techniques for an integrated approach to healing and spirituality. Her goal is to blend science and psychology with native lore for a path to happiness. IlgaAnn was given the Native name Spider Spirit Woman because, like the spider, she is a messenger. She is a professional speaker, trainer, spiritual coach and author. IlgaAnn holds a Masters degree in social work from the University of Denver. She is also an internationally registered Bach Flower practitioner and Bach Foundation approved teacher.

IlgaAnn is a former refugee and a naturalized citizen from Latvia. She survived living on the front lines of a war zone and has had several near-death experiences, including a head-on collision at 60 mph in a car whose engine was in the trunk. Her work experience ranges from being a waitress, to a radio talk show host, newspaper columnist, and business owner. Prior to her retirement and new career, IlgaAnn did crisis intervention work through the State Employee Assistance Program, in addition to managing Colorado's Drug-Free Workplace program.

IlgaAnn resides in Colorado along with two spoiled cats, Wolfie and Mooshie. She was widowed as the book goes to print. Visit www.legendlessons.com to read about IlgaAnn's journey on overcoming death, grief and loss.

Contact Information

- Sponsoring a presentation, workshop, or event in your area.
- Scheduling radio or TV interviews.
- Participating in our "Spirit Wisdom" teleconferences or teleseminars.
- For a calendar of upcoming workshops and presentations by the author, plus future information on new CDs, books, consultations, and other materials, please visit the blog.
- To order books please visit the website, Amazon.com, or your local book store.
- For a personalized, autographed copy, contact the author directly. Price: cost of the book(s) plus $5 shipping within the United States for the first book and $2 for each additional one.

I'd love your feedback, here's how to contact me

(however, I cannot guarantee a personal response to all contacts because of my busy schedule):

Firelight Crystals
P.O. Box 22832
Denver, CO 80222-0832
http://www.AncientSpiritWisdom.com

http://www.legendlessons.com

CPSIA information can be obtained
at www.ICGtesting.com
Printed in the USA
LVHW090717290520
656498LV00006B/212